Alashka

Janet Rodney was born in Washington D.C. in 1941. Her father was killed in the Pacific War in 1942. At the age of nine she moved with her mother to Paris; there followed a lot of travel, learning languages, different schools. About half of her school education was in French. Her mother remarried; they moved to Taipei, then Spain. In Madrid she worked as a reader for publishers, as translator, interpreter, editor and journalist. She left Spain in 1974 to go to graduate school, where she met Nathaniel Tarn. They married in 1983 and later moved to New Mexico. In 1987 she founded The Weaselsleeves Press. Her work as a letterpress printer is in fine print and art book collections across the USA. Her publications include *Moon on an Oarblade Rowing* (2005), which brought together three previous collections, and *Terminal Colors: Selected Poems 1974-2005*.

Franco-Anglo-American poet Nathaniel Tarn was born in 1928 and educated in France, Belgium and England, obtaining degrees from Cambridge, the Sorbonne and Chicago; he emigrated to the United States in 1970, where he taught at American universities until his retirement. He now lives just outside Santa Fe, New Mexico. Although he is perhaps best-known these days as a poet and essayist, he is also an anthropologist, with a particular interest in Highland Maya studies and the sociology of Buddhist institutions, and is also a translator of the highest order (see above all his versions of Neruda's *The Heights of Macchu Picchu* and Victor Segalen's *Stelae*). His first collection of poetry was *Old Savage/Young City* (London: Cape, 1964), which was followed the next year by his appearance in the seventh volume of the Penguin Modern Poets series. Three more collections followed in London, during which time he also became editor of Cape Goliard and founder-editor of the remarkable Cape Editions series of seminal modern texts: poetry, prose, anthropology, drama, many of them in pioneering translations. After he emigrated, only two more collections—the important volume *A Nowhere for Vallejo* and the ambitious book-length poem *Lyrics for the Bride of God*—were to appear in the UK. Thereafter, with the exception of his Shearsman publications and one other volume, all of his work has appeared in the USA, most significantly: *The House of Leaves*, *Atitlán/Alashka* (with Janet Rodney), *At the Western Gates*, *Selected Poems 1950-2000*, *Ins and Outs of the Forest Rivers* and the recent *Gondwana*. There is also a significant volume of essays in *Views from the Weaving Mountain*. Tarn's work is remarkable for expansiveness and its willingness to absorb material from very disparate sources—in this, it owes something to the examples of Pound and Olson, but also a lot to the author's own anthropological training, his knowledge of other languages and his interests in areas such as archaeology.

ALSO BY JANET RODNEY

Atitlán / Alashka (Alashka with Nathaniel Tarn) (1979)
Crystals (1979)
Orphydice (1986)
The Book of Craving (1997)
Moon on an Oarblade Rowing (2005)
Terminal Colors: Selected Poems 1974–2005

ALSO BY NATHANIEL TARN

Old Savage/Young City (1964)
Where Babylon Ends (1969)
The Beautiful Contradictions (1969; 2nd edition 2013)
October (1969)
The Silence (1969)
A Nowhere for Vallejo (1971)
Section: The Artemision (1973)
The Persephones (1974; revised edition, 2008, 2016)
Lyrics for the Bride of God (1975)
The House of Leaves (1976; 2nd edition 2018 *)
The Microcosm (1977)
Atitlán / Alashka (Alashka with Janet Rodney) (1979)
Weekends in Mexico (1982)
The Desert Mothers (1984; 2nd edition 2018 *)
At the Western Gates (1985; 2nd edition 2018 *)
Palenque: Selected Poems 1972-1984 (1986) *
Seeing America First (1989)
Home One (1990)
The Army Has Announced That Body Bags… (1992)
Caja del Río (1993)
Flying the Body (1993)
The Architextures (2000)
Three Letters from the City: The St. Petersburg Poems (2001)
Selected Poems: 1950-2000 (2002)
Recollections of Being (2004)
Avia (2008) *
Ins & Outs of the Forest Rivers (2008)
Gondwana and Other Poems (2017)

*from Shearsman Books

Nathaniel Tarn
& Janet Rodney

Alashka

Shearsman Library

First separate edition.
Published in the United Kingdom in 2018 by
Shearsman Library
an imprint of Shearsman Books
50 Westons Hill Drive
Emersons Green
BRISTOL
BS16 7DF

www.shearsman.com

Shearsman Books Ltd Registered Office
30–31 St. James Place, Mangotsfield, Bristol BS16 9JB
(this address not for correspondence)

Shearsman Library Vol. 1

ISBN 978-1-84861-585-4

Copyright © Nathaniel Tarn & Janet Rodney, 1979, 2018.

The right of Nathaniel Tarn & Janet Rodney to be identified as the authors of this work has been asserted by them in accordance with the Copyrights, Designs and Patents Act of 1988.
All rights reserved.

ACKNOWLEDGEMENTS
First published in 1979 as part of the volume
Atitlán / Alashka (Boulder, CO: Brillig Works).

Contents

Part One / CITIES

NT, Paris, to JR, New Hope: 5/17/76	11
JR, New Hope, to NT, Paris: 5/18/76	12
NT, Paris, to JR, New Hope: 5/20/76	14
JR, Madrid, to NT, Paris: 5/24–25/76	16
JR, Madrid, to NT, London: 5/27/76	17
NT, Paris, to JR, Madrid: 5/26/76	19
JR, Madrid, to NT, London: 5/30/76	20
JR., Madrid, to NT, London: 6/1/76	22
NT, London, to JR, Madrid: 5/29/76	23
JR, Madrid, to NT, London: 6/2/76	27
NT, London, to JR, Madrid: 6/3/76, 09:30 Hrs	28
JR, Madrid, to NT, London: 6/3/76	31

Part II / THE ROAD IN

Out from Pennsylvania	37
Going Through the Gates	39
Western Rivers, 6/17/76	45
Hamma Hamma City	48
Cities of the Dead	50
Terminal City	52
Blood Bank I, 6/23/76	55
Blood Bank II	57
Gun Mouth, 6/24/76	60
JR/NT: Each to the Other	61

Part III / WHITE/OUT

Narrative of the Entrance to the Great North	67
July $4, 1976 Sevuokuk: The Flight	69
The Lake	71

The Dream	71
The Mountain	73
Bicentennial Ode	74
The First Men	76
The Ground of Our Great Admiration of Nature	78

Part IV / THE FOREST I 89

Narrative of the Great Animal	103
Pendant to the Earth	118
Narrative of the Heartbeat	125
So Long, the Kenai	129
Letter from Homer	133
Three Death Poems	135

Part V / THE FOREST II 143

Narrative/Invocation of, and to, the Place Klukwan	160

Part VI / THE ROAD OUT

Perimeter	169
Marching Orders	169
What We Have Known As the Northwest Is the Southeast	170
Oregon Coast	171
Redwoods	171
Tactic	172
Home from the Nightless Summer	173

Note from the Authors	176

Acknowledgments

Despite any kind of appearances, every single poem in this geography is a jointly created fiction and any resemblance between the voices you hear and real, flesh & blood authors is purely coincidental.

The fictional voices offer these poems to the real voices of several people, among whom they especially remember: Larry Ahvakana, Fred Anderson, Harry Bremner, Nora and Richard Dauenhauer, Ernie Frankson and his family, Andrew Hope III, Andy McKinley, Dwight Milligrook, Albert Ningalook, Melvin Olanna, John Oktollik, Simeon Ootillian, Jim Pepper, Ron & Joe Senungetuk, Willy Willoya, Rosita & Bob Worl.

And to the light-bearers: Ed, Mike, Richard, and Roc, who will know themselves.

And to the earlier geographers: Barbeau, Boas, Brody, Carpenter, Chevigny, Collins, Giddings, Gunther, Kraus, de Laguna, Lantis, Lévi-Strauss, Nelson, Ray, Spencer, Swanton and Workman.

* * *

Some of these texts appeared in the following periodicals: *Bezoar, Credences, Handbook, New Directions Anthology, New Wilderness Newsletter, New World Journal, Paper Air and Raven's Bones, Survival International.*

The Ground of Our Great Admiration of Nature was first published by Robert Vas Dias at the Permanent Press, London & New York, 1978.

Twelve poems from *Forest* were first published by Walter Hamady at the Perishable Press Ltd., Mt. Horeb, Wisconsin, 1978.

As we drove West, wasting the miles behind us willingly, putting great space between ourselves and anything that bound us to a place: the stubborn refusal of sentences to form, of the land to take shape, of the future to obey our will, as it had obeyed it up till now, the great land desiring to remain open, and unexperienced, refusing definition from the start, to be worked thru and thru, mile by mile, without complicity…

Unless, overbearing all other sound, conscious only of impending disaster, lost in its clouds and mountains: that insistent call, that name, howl in the winds rushing from pole to pole, the immense continent not impeding, a voice, woman's perhaps, a huge lamenting voice crying for no known thing:

I
CITIES

NT, Paris, to JR, New Hope: 5/17/76

Remember the morning
after the tourists had whooped it up all night
making a ruin of Pennsylvania
                      we sat in our forest
the one we pretend to own
                      (until about noon
when the tourists come back to claim it)
            and we listened to the birds
with our eyes closed
                    making time together
  outside of history?
It's the poetry going thru us matters I believe
                    not ourselves as poets
same as the life, bird to bird, season to season,
  not the bird itself.

Remember in future:
                      when you can't see the birds
close your eyes and listen—
then they will unfold their major gifts.
  As they work, going about survival,
they offer, for whatever purpose of their own,
                    those astonishing sounds
which give us meaning.

                  We heard that concert then
which had been kept from us all season
                by our "responsibilities,"
day of invisible music
                rustling up summer,
  opening the road.
"Thank God" we said, "we are going back
                to everything that matters."

Time of patience now, testing out
              our memory of roads once traveled
  further than night
in an air of crystals where the breath
      is multi-faceted as thought.
Patience hunts the poem.
             The poem surrenders, opening
a two-way mirror. Each life answers the other.

JR, New Hope, to NT, Paris: 5/18/76

Answer a poem.
Only this one
wasn't dialed.
The door opened
I stepped inside
& found your message
on the floor.
Answer.
I mean, a half
of what I say to you
comes from you.
& I trust you
to make the connection
when I don't, I rely
on your intelligence.

People used to write letters.
They would get up early and write.
While their minds were fresh.
Set the day straight in writing.
Wire the day with words.
A diary for someone other.

They would give away
their best mind
and still have time.

Just as
there's light
at both ends
of a tunnel
& we carry this bulb
from one end
to the other,
I thought,
when I picked up yr. note
this is a light
transmission:
moves so fast
it's invisible,
moves so slow
it's invisible,
a feather passing
over skin,
the gradual brightening
of male plumage,
the order of seasons.
What are you doing now?

Each summer I
start to record
my dreams.

We were
sitting in a chair
back to back
with a double face
& through our mind
a movie flashed
of changing shadows,

we both could see light
but at different ends.
I turned to say—
but you weren't there,
you were
at the back of my mind,
eyes staring out
of my crown,
pulling me
towards the light.

NT, Paris, to JR, New Hope: 5/20/76

I sit at one of the crossroads of the city
which is itself all one crossroads of the universe.
Born here: so as to speak.
                No stone has moved, n.b.,
          the spirit-city still
                    in essence
         inviolate.
First station of the cross,
                morning after arrival
gas-chambers monument
at the tip of Notre Dame:
   "They went unto the ends of the earth and they
                did not return."
I had waited years to see that.
   We have been, returned,
                and are going again soon.
Later, at the *Laboratoire* for social anthropology,
   fall nose to spine with the British Columbia collection.
Lévi-Strauss has seen at last, I am informed,
                the Skeena's mist-skirts.

      I fly the Alashka flag among crowds
half of which carry the flags and patches of other nations
and are far too busy doing that to care about AK.
      I meet with Jacques Roubaud
who will walk three months from Minnesota to Louisiana
         setting his spine on Mark Twain's rock.
   We might send him a postcard as we cross?
The correspondences cannot end, not if they tried to.
The center is just another margin of another center
           bound by whale bones and beach ridges
         stretched like time's bow
      behind the arctic sea.
               Giddings, Louis:
homage to that man who dug us in
   thousands of years into the past, back of
first tattle of trekkers hunting land
   when all they had to do was stand still.
          And did. So as to speak.

The girl at lunch gets up, over and over,
           stoops on her lover
   so as to show the breasts in her open blouse.
I eat her breasts, among my salad, which is what she wants
        and miss your body language.
(Besides which, it is all good cannibalism, within custom.)
   Tonight, the Deutsches Requiem at Notre Dame
      with my lady mother, city-born also,
who comes here to wake her own mother
      lying between death and sleep,
         the small, cold waves
     bearing the birds of life
           on the swell of the Bering Sea.

Tomorrow, I read my poems on the French radio
     in this language I first spoke—
chatting with dear Deguy and Claude Royet-Journoud
               about Alashka.

And, of course, every night, the Seigle, my second parents
who love me from my twenties. My fellow student Chiva too,
and Lucien Biton, cook to the mortal mind,
    cousins and uncles also: Claude, Daniel, Marion.
While my mother's mother dies at one end of Paris
        and at the other end, another of her sons.

          Meanwhile I recommend
  our Pennsylvania to you as you wake
           since you still sleep there
six hours behind me on the waves of May
        among our wrens and orioles.
      Until our bones can buck the thaw
and freeze again in old
      yet still so virgin summer ice
and feel no pain, life draining out,
     as we return outside of human time,
                to the great bow
which draws the earth, and every nature in it,
        backwards to origin…
     I travel hard, with little company,
shuttle between the living and the dead,
     being of ice now, in my inmost thoughts,
and tho the world beats here with all its blood.

JR, Madrid, to NT, Paris: 5/24–25/76

Above the Atlantic
many miles high
imagine me
flying backwards
to that place between the ribs,
that warmest of

all hearts,
where they
bury their dead.
I suppose
the priest
told them to put up
a picket fence:
they took their slats
from the biggest tree.
& what better place
than a grove of
whalerib.
Different from this cage
skimming the tops of clouds
while somewhere below
you walk thru a door
or sit at the crossroads
where you have been lounging
these past days in my mind
in that last masque
you painted
of vegetable family,
packed in quilts
of ice.

JR, Madrid, to NT, London: 5/27/76

To be idle rich
not my wish
nor idle poor
but somewhere between
something parasitic maybe
unclaimed by gods or men

with time to do nothing,
or not.
As one chooses.
To engage the world
with time
to live & die
in doses
chosen at will
or letting either come
as it will
to do me in
or out,
to glide over
the mind's cities & woods
stepping through
the broken lights on pavements
or clearings
between your eye and mine
walking under the rains
within that fall,
leaving us dry as winter
ageing in our frames,
but with words to say it
& let them rise around us,
the words, and think:
"how they rise like a city around us"
or, "how they rise like a forest in our middle"
and watch them grow,
and watch us grow.

NT, Paris, to JR, Madrid: 5/26/76

This morning I heard a
            bird among stars
  Egypt was singing
              in the dark,
                    the king's
childhood sat under the falcon's shadow
who had descended from the sun,
                down ladders from the sun
and become, in the lower world,
        darkness.
                            —They

made these stones
        last some 3000 years
solid and earth-bound
        like his grandfather (Ramses's)
who writes the earth down:
        birds, all the names of
        birds & all the trees around.
                Fish in blue pools.
            Heat / heat. Far from
the ice-cap, bringing down the pole
                over the golden faces
of women longing at stars
        bulls, geese, hares
                plaited in their tresses…

            Do you know
                  how OLD we are
    to
speak to each other
        one in Paris / one in Madrid
            (under Velázquez light,
London between, later   Pennsylvania

and later still
>	departure in the dark
>	>	again towards that Pole?

>	Old with the world behind us
enough to have made ourselves
>	>	in our separation
cry to each other
>	taking in hand our sexes
>	>	each creating
from the rush of it
>	(brother & sister holding free hands)
>	>	an independent world…

>	>	And a world created from that.
>	My that and your this.
From the mixing of. My this and your that.
Nor woman/nor man. Bird. Fish.
>	Hinted at in former times.
>	>	Never more.

JR, Madrid, to NT, London: 5/30/76

This was my piece of Eden once,
the clear Velázquez air
& sky so close
to old stones,
rainworn tiles
sloping streetward,
lines clear
as your eye,
bells contrapuntal
music of the night,

clear, as your mind
among stars,
marking another time,
the falcon's,
his laser eye (like yours)
slept and woke
to sound of steps
going down
rung by rung
to darkness,
wings spread out like hooks
to draw up the fish.

But there's nothing
of innocence
here now, goes back
to a sound of laughter,
like water,
a hand churning
deep inside the pools
as fish leapt up
the ladders of fountains,
sun glinting off their scales,
they hit the sky
dazzling in their flight,
their migration north.

Now the Eden lies
like sun behind the rain,
when it comes,
revealing all the splendors
of darkness, its colors…

JR, Madrid, to NT, London: 6/1/76

From this poverty of nature,
all I can give you right now
is gold among the pines at noon,
    dark groves of the Meseta,
        their metal strings
           sighing above the trenches
where an army of brothers
assailed their brothers in the city.
      Today,
    flowers were exploding among nettles,
    each seed a parachute
    ready for the wind.
On that prow of land
I tend most afternoons
to drive out to with my Mother,
    pointing (like a ship)
    to the *Sierra de Guadarrama*,
        I stood like a mast
        as suddenly a gust
           rippled the grass
           and, sails full,
    I was borne off,
    Mother waving from the pier,
on a trip of discovery,
you and I back in Alashka,
        putting in at coves
    where high peaks veer into the sea
    & snow falls throughout the year,
           delicate lace-tips
           hardening on top
    while far below, the ice,
    softening under its own weight
begins to flow
and cracks in the surface

open and close,
    the whole mass breathing
       as it tramples over woods/lakes
wearing down/
building up
new mountains,
          gouging out valleys
          where the milk-carrying rivers
          deposit their sands,
              rubbing the earth's muscle
  with sun-golds, moon-silvers and ice-whites.

NT, London, to JR, Madrid: 5/29/76

This morning I found:
"…and they shall take down
the veil of the screen
and cover the ark
of the testimony with it
and shall put thereon
a covering of sealskin
and shall spread over it
a cloth all of blue…"
What were the *seals* doing in Israel I asked.
                For once the
rabbis couldn't answer.

Of all the outer masks:
the oldest operational again.
    I woke to watch my son ceasing to be a child,
wearing, on his shoulders, the shawl
    of all humanity, present and absent.
In his voice, a sorrow old as sand:

                    our people chased like rats out of the Egypt.
                                        This morning I heard the
Egypt singing, a
                        very sweet bird
I longed for, but I: (was ice, I came
                        to the sun and was ice.

                    In my tradition:
these men left Egypt
aeons ago—since then
leaving the home they found also.
Their aspirations have become
                        another home
                                        and the ice
has ceased to bother them.
                        They have no knowledge
    of solitude. The race dreams a home
    but Isaiah, Elijah, Ezekiel
                        are no longer among them.

                        They claim
the thing is live, moves, changes
but have no knowledge of change
or what could bring it about.
                    In their blindness
the poet-princes of Israel escape them,
they don't see them here.

                    This morning I heard
the Egypt singing, a
                    very sweet bird
        voice of sunlight, coming out of a pool,
                    turquoise, with goldfish veins.

Egypt was saying to the prophets
"Princes: unto you the song is given.
The exile which never ends is yours

                              and goes
beyond the desert, into the fertile land
and beyond the fertile land
into the desert again, but
this time it is a desert of ice
                    at the ends of
    known world.
            Where Egypt sings now, you would not
    believe it."

And the Diaspora went forward
    into eternity as such
is my take on us poets:
we are sundered / sundered and…
                        the world goes round
in never ending spirals, and,
we remain sundered / rootless / unhoused
    until the end.
When the Egypt sings, she has our voice,
        People of no country, flesh of the poets:
where Egypt sings now, you would not
                        believe it.

        I watch my son ceasing to be a child
with a coat of sealskin on his shoulders,
his voice rising into the rafters
            (to a drum he hears alone)
    holding up the house.
His voice keeps him alone,
the people fall off, drop back
                    into their secrets.
    My son rises on his own voice
                takes up the harpoon
    de profundis
from the cloth all of blue:
        they have mistaken for the sky,
            when it is the sea, mother of all,

when it is the cloth of waters
gave us our birthright
and the seal sings in his own voice
far into arctic nights
the race forgot to name
in the first days
when all was gold and silver
        white as yet unknown
asleep in the tip of the first harpoon
            floating in the ocean.

        We that are poor
and yet have riches beyond the dreams
of the men you and I know out there on the ice
at the very end of world!
           This morning I heard the
    Egypt singing
        a very sweet bird,
    all the inheritance of Egypt
    all arts and musics
      the gold and silver poems…
But the Egypt was no longer a center.

What is our poverty (in regard to the riches of Egypt)
    beside the poverty of those who are poor
in regard to us?
                What is it like
    that extremity of being poor
on the fringes of the wide skirt of the diaspora
    who is homeless to the end of time
        out there with her children
the children she has most lost
    in the blizzard, on the ice,
at the forward edge
of this thing which is supposedly changing,

that will not change, ever,
until all has been made sun-gold, or moon-silver,
      or ice-white?

JR, Madrid, to NT, London: 6/2/76

It is so good,
even in letters,
to keep the flesh between us
  and the poems happening always
  in amorous terms
    we both understand.
The meat of a rose
unfolding before our eyes
& as we enter it
  in a text so wide
  the whole garden
  rises & declines there,
we don't feel too much
the loneliness of a long day
spent apart in different lives,
  secreting words for an old world
  grown dim in its ways
    and far from that northern rim
    we've been leaning towards
    these past years, pushed out
      by centrifugal force,
almost driven, from that mythical middle
we call home.
  It is, I suppose,
  like water cascading down
    that never falls
or like the ice

on top of the globe
        that flows so slowly
        it can only be seen
               as still.
               And white.
We seem to move out
        from center to rim
        and back
               both poles attracting,
               unable to be still.

NT, London, to JR, Madrid: 6/3/76, 09:30 hrs.

Your three received
        (Alashka/Madrid), my own
London's out
        but, necessarily, the speed of light
around the world, into Pt. Hope, and back
not calculated for:
    some seizure in the data, something broke.
"It works! It works!"…
               Tha-
       lassa, Tha-
               lassa: we have reached
                       the sea
(too many musics playing, not sure
the subtlety of this is getting thru) but drafts, drafts
               against the future.

This morning
Kluane
               between your thighs
not knowing the mixture of waters

             white with the snows
formed by our bloods in drainage of each other
what degree of melt, into each other,
as when the river and the sea meet
and become one water
Kluane,
             Klu/a/ni
flowing thru my mind
& our feast day
             spreading the cloth of waters between us,
placing the food on the cloth
             birds in our eyes
rising, plunging,
             the bodies like ships
crossing in the night
     executing
             complex manoeuvres
around each other,
                      berthing
     BIRTHING
             because we are woman
                      & man
                             both with words.

I thought I would take the air
as it remains, stubbornly clear for both of us,
a kind of peace
             having descended upon us at the same moment,
the air: castile or île de france or thames
all one pale color, ice,
and, breaking it apart,
reveal our mouths, frost-rimmed, eating each other
and each other's words
as the totem-birds
in the night, invisible,
speeding over our cities,
carrying our thoughts
into each other's minds

               our desires into each other's
thighs,
      migrating,
          mixing the waters…
                  AND THIS BREAK, ing?

       It is a picture of mind
at work, you realize now,
nor idle rich, nor idle poor, but somewhere
                     in between,
to take, as I have always dreamed,
the whole world to one place & call both home,
the world melted into the place, the place
   into the world,
and why should not this be
those far, far, lots but, ah, untraveled so,
they stay so clear in the mind, so crystal clear,
      the mind can work on them, not be confused by
world so too much with us, as are now
these cities of the flesh we must transform:
                cities of intellect.

Yes, the wind blows
already over our bones.
We must find the
locus of those bones.
Life is the business
              death has with us,
it is nothing but
      a matter of
          recognition.
  And out of that the poem.
I'll hunt as never before.
There will be, among children,
        nothing like this child:
they will say the ice
      works miracles.

JR, Madrid, to NT, London: 6/3/76

> *"...and no craftsman, of whatsoever craft he be, shall be found any more in thee ... for thy merchants were the great men of the earth; for by thy sorceries were all nations deceived."*

 You can listen
  to the Egypt sing
  lucky you,
  but I hear guns
  & hoofbeats in the distance,
    someone riding all night,
    the wind in his cloak
    a cancer on his face
from Dover to Philadelphia
to break a tie
changing the course
of what?
   Sent Delaware to Revolution
    sent men to their graves
     sent England finally packing
in the name
of such a hackneyed tale
I don't have to tell you,
    you lucky,
    a bird in your ear,
    myth at least
    to make your day
while I
with my bestiary
of ancestors
listen to an ominous drone,
   looking for that mud
   not in the Nile,
   but the cantilevered nest
   sending down its cones

                    under our eaves,
our "promised land"
with its final sting
sending all hope,
all new-found things,
to market.
            You can say
            it's the Egypt singing
            but it's your voice
            I hear,
            giving it all a season,
                        joining all the oceans
                        or taking the whole world
                        to one place,
                your boy
                holding up the roof
                because you have been standing
                since he began
            holding up that roof
                for him with your song.
In my tradition:
    these men left England
    not so long ago
    and since
            have found another home
            in their sorceries
            with which they deceive
                all nations: and home
                        is what can buy
                        and what can sell,
                        all else in exile: how easy
                        it must have been,
                        far from land
                        to see the hills
        through which our Delaware moves,
        its birds of many kinds
        making their homes on its banks

    rubbing the air with their wings.
In spite of hardship,
 how easy
 it would be
 for those early travellers
   to change their course,
   an easy move upriver
   to a landscape as yet
     unspoiled by history.

Your song, not Egypt's
will stop the lynx, yes,
stupefy him in his tracks.
 the rivers will be silent,
 for a moment
 stop their flow,
   the wind
   will die down
   the leaves will be still
     & long after the ice has gashed our feet
     I'll remember your rhythm.
  how it speaks of a paradise
  where we could grow old together
    & where love can grow
   as the trees grow.
       far from the riches of Egypt.

The United States are about to descend upon Alashka.
On the ferry, as you sail up the spectacular coastlines,
there is nowhere you can escape the "Muzak." The Army
of consumers is prevented from realizing that nature
is more than just a moving window.

The tragedy of this State is that it is the last
in the Union (so far as we know) about to be "developed,"
this time with all the options known and documented.
Yet it is already defeated for lack of planning, lack
of faith where planning exists, lack of leadership and
above all a belief in monolithic "Progress."

Progress meaning: "more jobs, more people, more
improvements." There is no other notion of "Progress."
The garage man at Kachemak Bay told us of an oil prospector he threw out because of "overbearing manners."
Yet oil itself would ruin his town eventually. We can
be individual but not collective in our last stands.

The people who homesteaded here had solitude and
risk to dignify their poverty. Now the tidal waves
flood up, with instant "Culture," instant "Communications,"
instant "Betterment." Everyone is instantly rich. What
can the homesteader do but sell out and move on? For that
matter, where to?

II

THE ROAD IN

Out from Pennsylvania

Back from Europe:
        three days in Pennsylvania.
Is this a home?
Have we been to Alashka?
              Are we going?

Count-down
one hundred degrees
humidity atrocious,
twenty-four hours late
to a bad start
        packing out the house
packing in the world
        to the moving house
the van becomes
        on its rubber wheels.

Kitatinny Mountains: 15:20 hrs.

Not certain
whether ready for movement, or not—
moving again,
we must accept
movement as mind.
              We are not sure,
it seems to us, of time,
        whether this is a night
in the light of day,
        or one full of tomorrow,
dreaming of yesterday.
Travel
unravels all. We
come and go as we please
in the green dusk
        of Pennsylvania.

Tuscarora Mountain: 15:30 hrs.

Asleep in
the crook of Pennsylvania's arm
(the old positions,
familiar movements in the van),
we can become one another's poem.
Can we write letters to each other,
sitting side by side like this. driving,
lying side by side like this, dreaming?

Allegheny Mountain: 16:30 hrs.

Losing Pennsylvania,
passing into Ohio. Ravenna, Ohio: 6.12.76.
Campground as nighttime parking lot.
Attention, Ladies & Gentlemen, we are back
                      in the world of Nature!

Thick people
      beaten down by children
             eating thick food,
death already
      in their arteries—
             and this death
clogging the veins of Europe also,
      homogenizing the world.
    (There seemed moments to us
    when our cities could not breathe.)
                At least
  where we go
  we have space.
         Spots
    in which the leprosy
may not have settled yet. Europe, she chokes.

Later, a road-sign:
SIRES FOR ALL DESIRES
(American Breeders' Services)

Wisconsin: 6.13.76

Going thru the Gates

On the first journey:
gates of great country
begun far back,
gate after gate falling down.
Massacred Spring
turned to scorched August
in the weekend silence:
Pennsylvania rush,
Ohio gone by,
Indiana gone by,
Illinois—the
scramble of the skyway
into Chicago. Second day.
Dead pavements, wide roads,
empty of traffic,
riot of buildings
looming in the mist
of the crazed Summer.

The cranes at Sandhill,
fifth day,
refusing to rise on the wind
(costly for flight)
hidden in nesting coverts
among the rushing waters

at the far end of (invisible)
Wisconsin infinity.
Tornado, Madison, Wisconsin,
as we pass by.
roof torn off an apartment building,
a northern English voice,
soft in disaster:
I don't want this again,
I've seen it once,
never want to again,
don't like it here,
I want to go back to England.

We had always gone back to you,
daughter of *el gigante,*
dead swallow whipped
across ten thousand lakes
of forest Minnesota!
Immensity of the Mississippi
at Oresbach.
Be one of the new Minutemen:
Join the National Guard!
at Rochester.
All Motels and Hotels
adjacent to the Mayo
as the hotels are adjacent to
the gaming rooms you bet
at Reno and Vegas.
Gliders outside of Northfield, Minnesota,
last intimation of soaring
before we hit some rest.
Could you hear us talking
above the howling wind
which has nothing to stop it
between the frozen poles
on the way to yet another

thousand miles of heat and dust,
of crushing air?

The land unreeled from our fingers
below the wheels
like a green scarab
inching along the chocolate
prairies of Minnesota,
the thinly peopled
interminable acres.
We had talked, in Northfield,
of whether anyone
was rooted in this land
but had to know percents
of rural to urban
in order to decide.
Memo: discuss with Snyder
in Northern California.
Tenth day:
pond every half minute
in the Dakotas: each one
its resident waterfowl.
We thought we saw
a Yellow-headed Blackbird but
it went by too fast, or we,
and then we saw a harvest
of Yellow-headed Blackbirds.
There were tornado watches,
the skies
became interesting for the first time
during this trip
which was already, it seemed to us,
most interminable.

The girls at Skelly's truckers:
Aw, I thought you only

flew to Alaska! Envy
gravelled their voices for the rig.
Trucked on and came at last,
after days of swaying,
over the Plains, days of sweat heat,
mirage and waterfowl,
headwinds like walls—
more like sailing a boat
or plane, swaying from side to side,
bucking and slithering,
dodging the giant rigs
thru the deserted Republic
on a Memorial Day
no one remembered:
to the spinal mountains.
Down song of meadowlark
over the rushing waves of Sakakawea.
Meditation in the curtained rig.
Marsh hawk, harried by smaller birds.
Big sky over Montana harsh and louring.
Our old Wyoming
warming her tits to the south.

Thirteenth day. Down from Glacier,
Spruce grouse entering Alberta.
Pintail everywhere.
Waterfowl up like a tide
from the south,
homing into small waters.

Tribes all over the map:
what a reunion to be,
in the fall, back to south!
Suddenly, in the rig,
half-dozen bulky Bloods,
lead woman drunk a little,
claiming us for tribes

we had not heard of yet,
marrying us
to all her children one by one.
We say: we were married once
to these children, one by one,
we knew the tribes: we were priests once
and knew the rituals by heart—
tho not these skins, these pipes,
but others—south of here.
Insisted on leaving us their names,
each one by one,
small parchment,
treaty of some kindness,
having taken them to Fort McLeod
where they wished to go.

Consumer madhouse at Calgary.
Population of goods, a birthday sale:
these goods buy men.
The wind was saying
among the mountain pines
beautiful things in its own name.
Trails led off
into the wild.
Dared not quite go.
The sun beckoned
our feet to Sundance Canyon.
Pine smells, almost to sickness.
Twittering juncos
softly among the pines.
Rumor of grizzly, very far up.
Priesthood on high
where even the wind stopped singing.
Now: Banff, Louise and Jasper.
This is all one land,
borders are meaningless.
Country to country; state to state:

meaningless. The animals begin to reign.
Idiots rush at them, gaping,
clutching cameras,
hands held out, offering bread.
The animals are invisible.
Riding invisible Indians,
invisible national parks,
invisible eclipses. Moon over Sakakawea,
in full eclipse: behind cloud.
Sunrise, over Lake Louise:
invisible, behind cloud.
The people: invisible.
Louise, the fourteenth day.
Eleven more days to Anchorage.

Were we really going to the great land?
Would we ever see the ice?
Would there be freshness?
Eagles? Would our souls fuck with it?
Would there be polar bears, body to body?
Which was which now, would there be whales?
Which would be the faces
we would have to speak to
on pain of dying perhaps?
Held the wheel north—the wheel unwilling,
hours bending it to north.
Her name: all that was left of her sound.
We would be old when we got to the sea,
old, smelly, unrecognizable,
she would have nothing to do with us.
When we got to the sea, would she touch us?

Western Rivers, 6/17/76

      We're finally getting back
      to everything that matters:
      reality
of Western rivers
jerking seaward
that grind us like the dead,
                our silence
                below the ripples,
                another world
                flowing thru ours
          as we drive past
          our own shades,
          a woman and man
          receding in the mirror,
      we watch them
      look back at us
                and suddenly the rain
falls like arrows
aiming gleams & notes
into the moving fields
        and piercing us
        we fall too,
        grafted together,
              one body taking root
              and trying to remember
              with *all* the senses
                    what we only see.

Dandelion flowers
in British Columbia
become Provincial Flower
for the spring

on a patch of ground
out of Prince George's city
become our home for three days
as we waited for summer
to come out of the ground:
the raving sunburst of the flower
when queen of all it surveys—
there must be a lesson
in weed-triumph, "ugliness,"
as it turns to imperial beauty.
Quiet conversation among
quiet people ready to go
along with summer
wherever it goes:
not force it—don't push
the river, it flows,
all by itself.
The cat at our thighs
choosing us as all cats do,
this one actually looking
over our shoulders as we wrote.
Ah! sexual cat,
let's say, without verbiage:
pussy in the face.
Summer long days
which never ended,
flowers and humming wires:
they were bulldozing down
small towns as we drove in,
you could buy a town for a song:
fifty years from now
they'd be spending a fortune
building their replicas.
Photograph the wood, windows, doors,
get the details down
before they go down.
In the Canadian Legion,

bulldozer men stamped like bulls
on the night of our party,
turning women to cows,
bringing them down
with hot leers.
Years of concerted insult
paid off as old world courtesy.

Prince George, B.C.,
pines, birches and space
seeping in,
time occupied
the path we followed,
the river running with us,
& dandelions burst
into small suns,
at mile zero,
Dawson Creek,
a boy arched in,
overfriendly,
at the window:
spent my first
twenty-four years
in Doylestown, Pennsylvania,
now live in Alaska,
I see you have
Penn plates,
you wouldn't be
heading that way?

Hamma Hamma City

Driving around
the gods' peninsula
                Olympic,
rimmed with dereliction.

The mind like a pet
    wild on its leash
running around the circles
    of its privileged places
remembering the loci
    of its treasure hoards:
an art (unspoken)
        of memory…

The message goes
    from me to you,
now I carry the words in my mouth
    now you carry them,
the poem
    runs between us
like an invisible animal
    thru forest trees
leaving wild wakes
    ferns lying low
glazed with the sweat
        of its passing.

We are
among the trees
suspecting
    this is the blending place.
Blake sd.
    city,

Olson sd.
      city
and city is no doubt
         man's nature
  work's crown,
      yet
we wd. have the forests
         with a thousand hands
engulf the city
      not to strangle it
      altogether
      but to purify
      the buildings
      of all base
      proportions,
      weed out all those
      not fit to live
         with trees.

Rain all day.
After a walk,
after brief sleep,
      sunlight:
we might see the mountains.
      The sun shines
      the white daisy
      smiles in answer
      every creature
      has its right to life,
      the mountains appear
      from their cloud capes
      like brides
      at a mass wedding
      with the sun,
      pine and fern
      turn from grey to green

        those who spoke of light
        remember us as stars
        their thoughts
        falling on us
        in benedictions
        as we exchange
        our sexes with each other,
        the day is saved
        from ghosts and darkness
        it is set in the books
        of record forthwith
        and the bird rises
        to become an angel
        of our joint life.

Waktikeh Creek: 14:00 hrs. 6.19.76.
A moment later,
                      overcast again.

Cities of the Dead

We carry as many people within
        as places
    as outer masks of past lives
            on the edge of definition
                  gesture/intonation
    as inner marks like bells at night
        tolling unheard by sleepers
            each quarter hour
    eyelids move fast as lightning,
closed, dreaming.

Watching
    the living ferried from Seattle to Bremerton
and Bremerton to Seattle
    while the sun goes down over the Olympics
and we wait to be ferried to Alashka:
        where are the dead being ferried to
                in our minds
    or those so far from us
                      under the sea
    they are assimilated to the dead
in every element of their bodies except
                that of fire?

    Fire spreads over the water
as the ferries ply over Puget Sound
    and the dead come close to mind
        restless and unforgiving.

        The cities of the dead.
Death ploughing thru the middle of them
    sinking our families in its wake.
Leaving a furrow thru the middle of the living cities,
    (everyone dancing around it)
    over which the darkness settled,
        in the middle of which our families lay down.
Our families like broken trees,
        like scattered armies,
    fallen giants on Olympus flanks,
and we: still too young to carry the burden

        of their speech of fire…

Terminal City

Woken at four abruptly
by the ship's loudspeaker
      we are ejected into the world
as if Haines really existed—
        as if there were houses to be seen
   and streets to drive thru
     and people living there
          in terminal city—
        (but not with terror now
since we know terror is buried below Klukwan
         & that the treasures
  are underneath.

     Two eagles over the bay.
We go in dream quiet
thru the vegetation
saluting the mountains
crossing the Chilkat
   and where the treasure village smokes
in the early light
   we make no attempt to enter
desiring nothing more
   by way of a deposit
         than understanding.

Mosquito lake,
     the magic place.
Later we will breakfast
     among enduring trees
loud with mosquitos
     before driving back into
the Yukon skylight.

For now, we fall asleep
in the sound of raven and warbler,
clatter of earth,
whispers of heaven.

Getting van & body
on the road sometimes
makes you want out
of the *periplum vitae*,
what in Hell
were we doing here?
Inasmuch
as for a time
it preserves us
from tedium,
the Yukon Motel,
mile eight zero four:
pubescent trees,
jittering with warblers,
the road-skin tight,
a banality of names,
each once a discovery
throbbing by:
Dead Man, Lone Tree,
Wolf & Cracker Creeks.
Keep The Yukon Green.

In a dream
of limbs floating
in hot sulphur springs
our bodies boiled
to the caw of gulls
bringing inland
sounds of the sea

as the sun gleamed
thru willows
& minnows shone,
small flints of light
under the boardwalk.
Our cock
nudged into swamplands
& we wriggled around,
opening our mouth
wide like a crocodile:
let's fish we said,
& swim in this bayou forever!
That very morning
we consented
by being silent
as it rained
over Liard River, B.C.,
mile four nine six
to shake out
our mind-made body, the track it made
the track it made
unfathomable as birds
in flight,
the shell that contained
the genitals
was the blue
of turquoise
& somebody else,
we imagined,
was bringing
a mind set on gnosis.

Blood Bank I, 6/23/76

We wonder sometimes
about all this travel,
fear blur of images
yet
    the boat creaks
    shadow passing over shells
    our forms on the floor,
    waiting for sleep
 silence in our bones
 waiting to grow
 larger than the sea
 or mountains that meet
 the sky around us,
waiting for it to happen
the crack of ice
breaking us,
    almost touching
    here on the floor
 between the seats,
 rolled in down,
 our body-bags
 waiting for something
like the hail that fell
that evening in Ohio,
small eggs outside our door
    and we held them an instant
    their perfect shapes
    melting in the hand.

What we touch,
it appears,
is doomed
 with neither world
 quite enough

    by itself
            like a pair of loons
            at Mosquito Lake,
            where we headed on arrival,
the two travelling together,
real and reflected birds
marrying into water and sky
            & the rain that fell
            as drops of light,
            shattering the illusion.

Mosquitoes take our blood
carrying us to forest & lake,
to live under water as worms maybe,
or to fly, as blood no longer,
            in wing or leg,
            tiny thorax,
            or energy of flight.

    Mile ten five nine:
    Kluane Lake,
    Dall sheep in motion
    on the mountain,
    white specks
    among conifers,
    intelligence on the rock
    high above; Horseshoe Bay
    frozen by morning,
    winds galloping
    around the van,
    our human module
    parked under pines,
    the mind taking
    nature's shape again,
    record of icefields

advance/retreat:
　　　tide of an ancient music,
　　　sound of topography,
　　　clash of crystals
　　　on the beach.

Blood Bank II

The things we leave behind us:
　　ancestral moneys.
　　　　　Stored in banks,
　　no more than excrement,
　　　　forefathers' words—
　　　　　　little more than sperm
wd. have served better elsewhere,
　　Lord knows: our own poems even
locked in their selfhood,
　　　　　　　　too loud in the chorus.

but this adventure now,
　　work　/　working
the mind set in motion
　　not by wheels only
　　　　　　but by reunion
　　of primacies divided:
　　　　　　　　ANDRO / GUNE
pure, alchemical water
　　to save the planet
from mental garbage
　　(polluted airwaves)
　　　　　—not cities of the mind.

Our body risen
shown on the radar:
        AND THE CITY HERE
out of our bones:
    as child,
        as new moon,
            as ice-bow along sea-front:
                the city here,
old/new Atlantis.

        Bah! world is tired,
city
    chokes.
        The forest
is no model for habitation,
        but a barrier
            hacked into.
Raven flies further
        on the ice,
forgets the cities
        he has never seen,
forgets the ice he sees now,
which is the same as the ice he will see soon,
    remembers only dimly
where trees and towers met
        in an idyllic setting
Cook might have stumbled into
        or Fuca, or Vancouver.

Meantime, the latest bank branch
            raises its buildings
in bids to make our money happy,
        stuffs the city's throat
    with bank notes

sends *Androgune* on her way
        with nothing for food or gas
           EAT / FILL UP / SLEEP
because they don't cash
        out of State checks
               in Alashka…

    At four o'clock,
    mile one two two one point three,
    we crossed a boundary,
    moved an hour back
    as we drove forward
    into Alashka, the ghost
    of Mount Sanford
    soon floated towards
    Gulkana & Anchorage:
    on the road
    above Matanuska
    a glacier's snout
    pushed thru gravel
    as far as the eye could see,
    mountains and
    moonlike scars,
    and long waters flowed
    far beneath the ice,
    cooling the waters
    of the mind.

Gun Mouth, 6/24/76

We think we hear
but noise blocks out
the half-sounds seeping thru
                      the
                      ticking of a clock,
                      like a bomb
                      carried these past weeks

        only now,
        three thousand
        miles later,
        it comes to our attention
                that having crossed
                four time zones
                we're ready to aim
                for another,
like spruce time or
ice heaving down the mountain time
or, in brutality of silence,
the wearing down of rock time.
                We have to know how
                to slow down
                enough to imagine
                what we know is happening:
we become a glacier,
    withdraw & break out as spruce
                at the bottom of the sea
                we watch the ridges
                form on our backs,
our mind carving
its way thru the block.
    We listen to the deep tones
    of voices spinning
    cedar into wool,

    the warp of time
    winding thru
    index & thumb,
& knowledge of silence
flows from behind
the scheme of things,
    the sutures of our passage
    thru a gunsight
    where the birth waters break
from behind our mouths
  inevitably made
    to eat this earth some day,
& we give birth
that morning
in complicity
with all the elements,
    becoming the many faces
    of the land this moment of
     our re-entry.

JR/NT: Each to the Other:

  Head into the wind,
  hit the road again,
  swing round the pocks,
  there are many
  to catch a wheel upon
  and only two of us.
  Go, and there is no spare
  to put in your stead
  we didn't foresee
  what would happen
  if I should unbolt:

you would inherit
backpacks, sleeping bags,
portable stove, tent,
you'd drive on
to new lands
holding to the fantasy
of discovery
while I bounced thru
a lunar landscape,
unbidden as the blast
of a fallen star,
one more crater
for you to cross.

For architecture to be beautiful, a people has to believe in duration. A city is designed to stand for a thousand years, perhaps for all time. The buildings also have to suit—in shape, size, materials —the prevailing climate, tame it to man's needs. When technology is "instant" and when the future is seen as uncertain or uninteresting, there is no need for architecture. Provided it is warm, or cool, a house, a senate, a cathedral, can all look like, or be, quonset huts.

The destruction of the Californian coast is accomplished. A leprosy spreads from San Diego to the Oregon border, or will spread as soon as the pressure gets strong enough. Wherever oases have not been established, the coast from Oregon to Alashka will suffer likewise. It is a matter of greed and time, both of which are plentiful when time means nothing.

The Native habitat was an adequate response to the Alashkan environment. So was the homesteader's hut. As things are now, nothing between that and a visionary architecture is an adequate response. Anchorage and Fairbanks have sites fit for angels to live in but los angeles have already been shipped or airlifted up the coast.

The great land can only hope that it will defeat man yet by being so great that it can never be found.

III
WHITE/OUT

Narrative of the Entrance to the Great North

Pow/   here is the great American promised
    land with
              mountains of light bursting apart
the frosting air
                      light-on-light
and pow/
      the gates
           at whatever cents an acre
    from the Russians,
       the satin air
shot with mountain bluebirds
the bluest bluebirds ever
the purest air
       a mystery of mountains
             where Canada ends
veil after veil, gate after gate
       as the sun slants—

Land of no night
gone beyond where night is known
past the hot Liard, rush of Yukon
two thousand miles into the Bering Sea:
all your peoples, North, crying:
       "want moose, want bear,
         want wolverine, trickster,"
on other side of the crest,
hard over St. Elias,
Yakutat, friendly Thlingeet:
       "want green over this,
         want bluebirds on the snows,"
Queen of the Yukon, sister to the Spirit:
       disappeared forever
         among eagles, lynxes,
         among snow-births…

Three Dall sheep
    pure ivory, telescoped on Sheep Mountain
as if by royal command.
    Mist over the water,
        a thousand miles of dust
            sinks to the bottom
    of Lake Kluane:
no sediment,
    weariness dropping off
        like antlers,
presenting oneself cleansed
            at the great gates.
    We climb into woollen pants
against the zero
    into the van now baptized "The Yukon Ritz"
        drinking Moskovskaya 100° by the pint.

Summer foods on
dashboard table, against the zero:
    bread
    mayonnaise
    tomato
    cucumber
    scallions
    cheeses
    banana
    broccoli
plus central heating vodka
    against the zero.
        Outside,   thrashed by the wind,
catkins not seen so thick since polar Russia
        their woollen outerwear gross among lupins.
    And who'd have known as well
that Alashka would be full of swallows!

Pow /   that asshole
Robert Service,   "Bard of the Yukon,"
    is discontinued:

hasn't anyone been around lately
        to open Kluane?
What passes for a poet up here
        is Robert Service:
they probably needed you, William Wordsworth,
with a dash of Walt Whitman in you
and the spunk of an Arctic singer,
    Siberian shaman perhaps,
    St. Lawrence Yupik. Notes made,
against the zero
                for an
"Ode to WWs in the great land."

Morning. Sunshine after the storm.
(had howled and whistled all night long the worldling
                              wolves…)
Ice against shore, large crystals
        rocked by musical waves.
The blue is astonishing, a knife cut.
Two pair of Red-breasted Mergansers
        dipping close to shore—
then lightning flight against the ice.
Spirit of the North : the path zips open.

    Pow/   trip-totems found!

July $4, 1976: Sevuokuk
The Flight

Riding above the dream,
    above China, above Japan,
        with the wind
coming off the mountains of Siberia.

The Old World at its closest.
    We could touch its tail
before it sounds into the deep.

        Back at the airport
our cities had been coming and going,
British, Lufthansa, Air France, Royal Dutch
    among the local traffic.
We had stopped on our way
    at several stages of the city,
        each one a resting place
            further from "civilization."

From the plane:
    sparkling day, bergs like fungi,
green keels below blue water,
    giant tattoo on ocean's face
looking past us at the sky,
    whales with spouts like kettles,
a procession of imperial animals
        blowing north.

It is as if we had no pilot,
    the plane were rudderless,
understanding our intentions of itself,
        all morning long
we run before the wind,
        upon arrival find
total exhaustion.

This is where we get to,
people fluttering on the shore below,
black and white flash of snowbird
        foretells our arrival:
wings like a mask in our minds
    of night and day fused
        under covering wind.

We have come to the ends of the earth
   by the thread that spins for us
      the long carpet of blue
         unrolling
               from pole to pole.

The Lake

Seas rage. Livid light.
   In the dream,
      we have walked 200 miles today
around the mile-long lake
over gravel dunes,
      sphagnum moss, water-logged birds,
   shrill signals of alarm,
and, along the lake—
      last ice decomposed—
               a diaphanous wind
pushed up tiers of flutes and organs
           playing Aeolian tunes.

The Dream

Asleep in the half light
   not knowing night from day,
      or whether to be hungry—
heads full of light shards
      watching the sea
     stroked by a Russian wind .

Out of our knowledge of each other
        strangers in us
      reach out arms we recognize.
Hair howls as night nears
    (or what approximates to night):
        whether to sleep again or wake.

          It pours out of us
the music,
    ice scales playing
          the fire also,
    sleep rounds the door,
          seeps thru storm windows,

the lowering sun
    leaps thru a cloud-break
lighting up whaleribs and boats
           awash in the twilight
    we look out into
        with sleep-studded eyes
and feel the frost coming for us

      inside these barren walls.
We hack at the ice
    with a bone chisel,
          stagger about,
    converse in this house
which is as of the dead,
a cavern at the top of the world.

We learn precision from the wind,
    murre racing round the island,
        puffin and auklets, bullets
    in tight, windborne formations,
           putting on an air-show.
The snowbird plays outside the window
    inkspots/ivory,

    his song still hovering
        over the stones.

Pieces of paper fly up the beach
  except for one going the other way:
we laugh: it is the bunting again,
   our mask careening on the wind,
        dark eyes staring in.

The Mountain

Yesterday
  the sea
    with thunder fists
battered the shingles
  dissolving into musical
    lace among stones.
      Today the waves
     bring in a radiance
   as of other seas
(cloud layers dissolving
into astonished blues
  as of
lagoons far to the south)
     does not belong to them—
    borrowed for a day,
        this idyll
    suspended from the sky
    above the beach
      picks out the hunting boats,
      bones along ridges
        exposed to light.

    The sea a moment
             seemed to cup us in its hands,
                 lifting us,
        and fed us up the mountain.
Came to a place, wet underfoot,
           high crag, snow-covered,
where we could stand
         and looking back, see Sevuokuk,
              and looking forward, see the whole island
                    up to Savoonga—
then, swivelling,
      in slow arc round,
           welding Alashka and Siberia,
               their mountains in one blow:
re-uniting worlds,
           beach of stars and planets
                rolling under our feet.

Bicentennial Ode

Next day
        the sun doesn't shine.
                It is snowing at 4 a.m.
                      out of Siberia.
We let the morning ride,
      grey whales still spouting out to sea,
                light glinting
as they play unhunted along the coast:
            "our domestic pets."
The bunting forages under the door,
     the silence is magnificent
        broken only once
by a radio crowing "John Brown's Body."

    Occasional clatter of a three-wheeler.
                      We let the weather clear.
      Rare gift of leisure:
      to be idle rich,
    when a man and woman get up,
      look at the snow,
    settle into reading or writing—
allowing the weather to improve.
        The people gather in celebration.

What better than a Birthday Ode
    on the fourth of july here in Sevuokuk,
        (Nome radio spewing yesterday
        last list of frantic details—
        presidents, generals, bankers,
        facts of the shallow case.)
In the dream wind it will not matter,
      tho the people were cleaning up the village
and lighting bonfires.
Where else should one be on such a day
      but among the only people
        to live in both old world and new?
From here the Mainland's bicentennial seems
                faintly ridiculous.

      "Footraces for all ages."
        The one-year-olds stumble
    towards "achievement,"
      watched by four smiles,
    tattooed old women—
        last of the arctic—
    jacknifed forward on bowlegs,
      calico parkas, faces melting.

Scattered fireworks
    with no night to explode in
      bursting blue flowers on the bluer air.

                In the brilliant light
a billion auklets wash and dive,
    the whale still spout
           calling their kin back to the sea
from their rotting bones along the shore.

The First Men

Moving across to the old sites
        (Collins and Giddings ravaged:)
trash fields of stone and bone
            smelling of mint
   we bring back order to
     a desecrated past,
imagining
    the first men arriving on a quiet day
            like this,
mistaking the snow for more home snow
and following an animal a little further than usual
and setting up a house to get away from a neighbor,
    passing from what was to become Siberia
into what was to become Alashka
    when there was no longer a land-bridge
      between the so-called old world
            and the so-called new.

And we ask again
    what is our poverty (in regard to
the riches of Egypt)
    beside the poverty of those
        poor in regard to us?
Our poverty is
not knowing that in such and such a place

             they owned land,
        that each year in camp
        the sea mammals were there,
        that even the whales came to them.
                    Not having knowledge
        of the land itself,
            recognizing all species
        of plants and birds,
            common or rare.
Our poverty is the romance of the North
as told by some,
                of a barren world
            men felled one after one
            on infinite, still ice
            by mutual distrust,
            loss, solitude, despair,
            frustration, drift—
    the ground they stand on
forever shifting
                like the sly fog come calling,
                    shows/hides the mountain,
while flags of laundry snap on the lines,
    and three small boys
        ride round and round
            the only sidewalk in town.

This is what we sd.
    but in our hearts,
which came to heel like hounds in this business,
    we knew the immortal white of the place
        is what we had failed to reach,
                knowing instead our minds
                in those of other men.

The Ground of Our Great Admiration of Nature

        I

The poet as the sole
        remaining speaker
    can now,
the whole, grown beyond reason,
   still speak of whole, but, now
as certain is to probable
        in other languages,
     the wonder—
mind shock : incompatibility,
        admiration,
wonder ever recurring despite
       the loss of doubt
   in that respect (considered as "beauty"):
her arms swimming, as if thru water,
the frontal surge of breasts, like frozen
    breathing
      at the apex—
       but / in fact / in air—
"too much language, too much language,
   too many games, now, with the language":
our positions almost lost
      unless it is not water
   she comes thru, at the apex
       but air
       residence of the purpose, the
   seeing,
   need for us still in the blood of the air
        (so thin now, leukemic…)
the mermaid song
   her tail, our desire, such a comet
       among air's trees:
   as if lungs were still

as if causally / pretending only,
                        but *required?*

        II

No more of that being
                no one
         but being all, in season,
           —y *con fuerza*, ok?
They have made, after all,
of beauty, a slavish thing, a handmaiden
                perpetually
to the other desiderata of thought,
         have reduced
the domain of our interdependence:
    where we chase
her thru the trees, as she herself
             once grew into a tree
and we had wanted (remember that?)
her skin until the very moment
               dry and sear
   it turned to parchment—
they have made
   yes, of that wood, paper, we cannot use,
books we can't bind
   or read in common parlance / they have not
allowed us to
   possess ourselves away in dispossession
     thus being lords of worlds and legislators,
         but tucked us into corners
hemmed us in,
         hacked down our hiding trees after
hemming us in—
           so I tell you
in the name of this rich soul (Fr./Sp.)
(this complete transformation of a people

          into a state):
        no more: *âme* / *rica*
of that being
        no more / ok? / *de grâce!*
Sweet virgin land:
            Havre   de grâce!

III

Tried:
    lifeless matter / lifeless God
or
    living matter   /   living God
                but, at the heart,
still (and unexplained)
    the snow like down for no known
            purpose and the ice
    blue on its faces like angel faces
        and then all this:
mosquitos drave men mad
    (oppressive to "savages") and
        great sea monsters filled with oil
the sake of food
    but we shall eat tonight? not eat?
    there shall be famine? or rich weeks?
            (the waiting)
    the waiting to go back to   grace's harbor...
      stillness of the man on the ice
        movement at sea
    the correspondence of desire and patience...
      Like a mermaid
           exquisite song (ears, ears)
    bunting by day
      owl-howl by night
           over the city of ice
                visibility down:

you cannot tell the houses from the fields,
    earth from the sky
                      and, when you go
        into her uninhabited
wastes no guarantee is given
                          the direction shows
    backwards to hope
        by ripple or by drift
                there's a way back...

    IV

Close to
            suspecting in some part
that wide and utter freedom, stroke of wing
                across the emptiness,
feather against the cloud
            tip of the void
forcing the lock
    like a key
        to fly beyond, into
the world we have before us now
            our eyes opened
on our hands before us,
        body below us
feet touching ground
    and it is:
           what, this earth? what, this
loam so fertile, it has a name, it is
    recorded in the early books
        / is it not?
    books which still speak
        union of dead and live
    where they have not let us go quite yet
        into the wings,
the screens, and hidden corridors

of the clouds—
    suspecting in some part
              that wide and utter freedom
I hear of somewhere, and am / so close to / sometimes
          it is almost as if
   (the great bones hug my soul)
somewhere at last I could
              sweet virgin land
   so nearly
        touch it…

              V

On the paradox:
         that the stars are unread,
   the winds unheard,
       the bird, poised between mind
and tree, out there among the winds and stars,
   is not to be declared
victor in war or peace / is not to be
              so far brought down
   close to our ear
       as to name music for the age,
on this scandal:
our realm is built
        imagine:nation, many thus
            its citizens,
all of us : dear relatives,
       (tho duty-feeble in that sense,
       brutal to each other, and sour,
       leaving each other in solitude
       cd. bring us close to death: AH!
          how hard it is to breathe!
but all that, all that:
       our private matter:

To you out there,
   this is a culture,
      civilization now
          outlaws the past,
sheer force of *fiat*,
   that it be, and that it be this way
the stars now read
         as they set dolphins dancing in her eyes,
and making perfect sense, a happy day
      in store for everyone
           and the bird out there,
a moment past
   (this shard of hope against my breast,
   growing a point)
        a moment past   mid/night.

VI

As for the
       point of balance, judgment
will produce:
   the artifact in splendor, this
is Point Hope.
      Above this desk, the victory
      towers in ivory, 3" high—
served to propel
the killing shaft towards the bird
     or seal or caribou
   "sufficient to the appetite of natives"
   (we found three carcases of owl)
          ∴ to purpose purposive.
   And I will kill
     the lyric as it soars
         by memory:
   all the lyrics before it / this is
      elegy,

        and, as the lyric dies,
same way the owls snow on the sea by day,
      on land by night
           wearing their fatal decorations,
the page fears for the newborn song while process dies
              and the snow pocks.
  The shaft falls off,
    the point lives on alone (Maryland, Maryland)
        a throb inside the prey
and then is dead to it
      and food to us:
               duckwood in the mouth, sawdust.
But in that moment, frozen,
   THE VICTORY
(400–700 A.D. precisely, "winged Object," man said—
   the white man did not know for once, "part of a sled"
      and sold for cents)
mounted: looks like her, headless,
         where the head,
   lodged in the prey eats at its life with teeth
        soundless as memory
triumphant as desire, this
    arching of the bones above the dead
(the rib-cage, containing the song,
containing the meat,
containing the meat we have made of the song
    as we devour our poets
KANNIBALISMUS!!!
     this as I said's)
  Point Hope, and all is

              possible…

VII

Archeology of Nature:
> memorials
of ancient mighty desolations
> man had no part in:
> mammoth-rut below starlight,
whale among icebergs,
> the purpose of our genitals,
> organization of love,
whereby all created things come to birth
> (and shall we say
> petrification being of
the order of A. of N., not
> history natural,
> stone has no say in purpose?)
But the very organ
set those same whale leaping thru Tongass
> we saw in admiration
as the sweet product of our ancient patience,
> has been, time past among,
> (among the icebergs)
a stone as well,
> so wood among the trees
with which the soul-cage used to breathe
a stone as well:
> if there be any trees
> in these cold regions.

The mind
> says it will do this:
> evolve from stone
> with all its gorgeous colors
setting the tundra quietly on fire
> beyond the night.
(little sparks of fire, like
> love in flame when life
> most hopelessly devours us).

We have come a long way
from the familiar eastern shores
                        to the ground
of our great admiration of nature
and we watch the greys
weave with the silvers and the golds
and the sands, and the greys again, out to sea
beyond the polar ice
which is the blue of angels' faces,
    when they are cold—as we say:
    COME INTO THE HOUSE OF OUR LIFE
    ye that have hugged the bones
    whose rib-cage is the whale
    that swallowed the prophet
    of the mighty sea. Crosses, crosses
now, above Point Hope, the shamans dead,
imagination buried
under the oval freezure,
           the petrified milk-drop
the bones, jutting into the sky like the teeth
of an animal more immense than the whale…

    Hold, hold to your patience
beyond these immemorial angers
        and she will fly into your poem,
               who are there
wearing her mask today, & breasts, beating her drum.

IV

THE FOREST 1

for the people of the tides

In that part of the mouth
where the dome reaches up
the tongue settles in silence,
breath blowing from far down
in soft gusts
that make the snow whirl.
There are strangers in our house,
come to look at our land
& take our picture.
They do not want to meet us
and they will not stay.

For a thousand years
before we came
they lived inside the storm
inside the cloud,
the mist, the rain,
hardly ever came out
until we gave them the sun:
not every now & then
as a great feast to be remembered,
to be counted with
the centuries—
but as a permanence
they could not stand.
And they said no
and became
invisible

Down came the storm again
like a hood over earth's head
and ever since then
this region belongs to rain,
raven caw,
eagle screech,
and there is nothing we can do
to change it back.

Let's open this our home,
the poem, where doors
    are alive
    and houseposts talk
    & no property is allowed,
because,
    to put it one way
    nothing is ours
    & to put it another,
    everything is:

having got here by following
markers in the forest
the rainworn story
in perishable wood
of a people's passage
thru wet country,
poles of family legend
and the trees, our guiding texts,
from the largest library,
the forest.

It was a question of whether
we should bring Dionysus
to the Pacific
with a new name
or whether
I'd simply watch you
    (or you me)
    perform
in a new setting:
    your form

the closest,
most known & most loved,

as you perch on an offshore rock
    eyes moving
               fast as fish
darting in & out the waves,
your headdress of entrails,
the sea lions on your upper arms
roaring at the moon
    as a bird flies
               out of your mouth
your knees, faces
      talking to the stars, a frog
    covering your chest—
why not,
    if here also
I can choose a waterworn stone
heat it by fire
      while the tide's out

& give birth
to a slate-colored son.
Because these & all myths
are the very bones of poets
and our skulls are crusted
    with abalone
long before we are done.

"Not one of its former inhabitants was to be seen
excepting about fifty dogs
that were making a most dreadful howling."

What happened was
a glacier taking place
or a lagoon forming,
in either case,
canoes bobbing up
& down on tides
& shores along which
in winter many bears
in their sleeping holes
covered up so only
their ear-tips showed.
What happened was
summer grass
shoulder high,
an abundance of berries,
a town, its strand
(depending on one's attitude)
between the legs—or jaws—
of two headlands,
where
at low tide women visit
the lower stretches of the lagoons
gathering cockles,
sea urchins & clams.

You trace
with your index
an almost perfect circle
clockwise:
        life
is just as round as this.

Nothing to do but walk around
tho it's a long way
and risky.

That is your feeling,
of trudging around a bay,
of a shore curving
from birth to birth
it's just a feeling
but when you are young
you start out on this bay
& when the breeze from the old
(as opposed to young)
side starts blowing,
you begin to feel old
& act like babies.

And all the time
the land
helps you
find yourselves.

It happened
that sea otter took shelter
under cliffs in a storm,
families collected
hemlock in spring,
ducks stood
on top of the water,
shaking their wings.
It happens also
that a young man
runs his boat on the rocks
chasing his love
thru the dark
& a bear swimming,
at a girl's glance,
turns to stone.

Like the blues
poverty lurks
in your pockets
or under your armpits,
you tell your children
not to stand lazy
warming hands
in their pockets
or if there is no pocket,
under their arms
because poverty
lurking there
will suck their fingers,
they'll never
make any money.

Here are
rocky slopes
covered with alder
willow and fireweed,
here are
waters filled with floes,
seals stretched out on ice,
here
a man nearly fell
while hunting bear,
another set up huts
smokehouses, tents,
& hunted seal
while women flensed,
rendered the fat
& stretched the skins,
a third
brought in the seagull eggs
for omelettes.
Here camps were redolent
of seal oil
& the beach was white
with weathered bones.

She's a high class woman,
and this is a weight.

You want someone
to tell you a story
about a woman,
what you mean is
you want somebody
to teach you
the real life,
& everywhere you go
they start telling you
a story about a woman
so you get up
& walk out & on to
the next house
& the same thing
until finally a slave
tells you:
          "Never sleep
when it's stormy at night,
just keep busy."

You stay and serve the slave
like he is your uncle,
the slave becomes your uncle
and you his slave,
and in the real life
there's this story
about a woman.

One of your women married the Sun.

& here is where
ravens are overcome
by Russians going fowling,
where the print of a body
in the sand
is like one would make in bed
where two old women
lying in wait for Texans
are turned to rocks,
where families misplace
the hunting grounds
of the first salmon,
where hemlock and spruce
& wild celery stalks
no longer run with sap
& herring spawn,
seaweed and urchins choke
in the foam at the shore's lips,
the hunters sailing
up and down the bay, poaching,
canoes overloaded with seal,
where
beaches are raised by earthquake
& waves beating the bluffs
wearing a coat of slick
wash down the gold-bearing sands.

Your boys do not sit
on rocks, your boys
are ready
to get up at any moment,
squatting on their heels.
To sit on rocks
makes slow & heavy hunters,
your boys spring up
like sapling
take a cold bath every day,
even in winter
till they're stiff.
Your boys do not drink broth
from another man's kill,
nor do you
ever drink
too much of anything
because things
that flow to you
will also flow away
if you drink too much
of anything.

Narrative of the Great Animal

            I

Denali was our greatest animal.
We might   never have seen it, doubted
all reports, never realized
         why it was unmistakably
lord of America.
            It rose, when it rose,
two whole days
    out of surrounding mountains
         like the sun's ghost
after a burial at sea,
         like the white
whale
out of the sea
     defining all else immediately.

Almost a painting.
   That unreal: as when they say: "postcards,"
                                           etc.
         (or "travel poster.")
Archetype of all mountains,
        behind the mind, lurking,
no: they say of a *beast* "lurking"
  and we talk of gods.
Always there, against: the epiphany.
       White ship of space, rootless,
suspended from the clouds.
        Sometimes, the whole sky grey,
the crown, floating by itself in the heights / or /
      clouds on its face: recessing it,
into immeasurable farness,
      or lifting it (the mountain) / depressing it,
according to the play of cloud.

                    A RESURRECTION,
                                        from the dead,
from the death of our senses, in its shroud,
which is also a wedding gown:
                    bride / bridegroom
                            in one plenitude.
Knowing, or not, the plenitude: there is
                                        no other question.
(That we could have been, again, encamped,
with most of humanity at the foot, and spent
days,   days, weeks even,   and not seen it /
as so many, coming all this way,
on little money, their poor lives spent,
at the gates now, and, *still*, not seen it:
this   beats   all   matters   of   election,
and Mallarmé's absence, or Kafka's gatekeepers.)

                    When, thus, it rose,
and we, disbelieving, who had said
all along the way
            "Is *this* Denali,
and then this, and this, and this—
                since there is no end to
    the mountains
                but, patient: there being always a step below
    suspect perfection,
                until, at road-curve,
"Oh My God," hushed, and you not seeing yet, and then:
            you also:
"oh my god," in a still greater hush,
    because, now, there was
no possible mistaking.

                GREAT STAR OF SPACE
from the dead
    complete,
            in its motionless travels,

even then: at its destination, never yet gone
                              from earth, its
              parent. We might not
      have seen it, never
              have looked on god's face
and lived (so far) to tell tales.

                      Had we not
      seen it,
      the world
      would have always
      forever thereafter,
      and its word, *logos*,
seemed smaller   because,
              after the moon, after all,
      it is never the same again:
an earthly thing has to be great indeed, perfect indeed,
                  to give that plenitude / that lack
      of argument, tells us we have
                      looked on god's face
and lived (so far) to tell tales.

And, had we not seen this,
would not have seen, either,
in any sense of the word "seen,"
since only this mountain gave the world eyes
                              and senses
to apprehend it with:
              (catalogue / world model):
              the cinnamon mountains,
              all the other mountains
              in their variety,
              the heaving bears, with earth
              like Atlas, on their shoulders,
              wolves, running fast as cars,
              our idiot ptarmigan, posing at roadside,
              the payroll animals, bowing as each bus passes,

                    the tourists shouting...
                            (continue at own leisure):
        my-minute-preoccupations
under Denali:
        horned lark (American first)
        eagle (repeat); eagle (but immature)
        wheatear (American first)
        phalarope (American first)
        (continue as per notebook,
        list climbing, x% of total record).

                        But the invisibles:
                            harlequin duck (later: St. Paul)
                            arctic warbler (later: Point Hope)
                            golden plover (later: Shishmaref)
                            ivory gull (later: Gambell)
                            gyrfalcon (later: Nome)—
                        all these,
                        waiting for the next time,
                        the world being in place now,
                        no problem.
                        And seen, then, again and again,
                        the lord Denali,
                        from: Turnagain Arm, Cook Inlet,
                        from the roadside, on the Fairbanks highway,
                        from the plane, out of the Pribilofs,
                        as if it were a friend now,
                        and reluctant to leave...

and the great animal,
even greater than *this* animal,
(Denali god-beast,
with hips of stone
and rock-haunches),
        waiting for the next occasion also
to get us before another sighting,
        another chance at this vicinity

among the thorns and dangers of this world—
BUT WE HAVE SEEN IT
and thus, by implication, also the other:
as dark as this is bright...

Cloud of mosquitos,
Splat: blood on hands, face, clothes:
wolf / moose / bear / bird blood perhaps,
John Doe from Texas, or Oklahoma blood,
                              ("the animals")
What a merger in the sight of the whole!

            Outside the Park, every signpost in Alashka is
                        riddled with bullet holes,
            the land should have never seen people
                        this blight on it:

    back into civilization...

            II

We could not remember its form
                        (the mountain, woman now)
dropped from high cloud
                on memory,
mind's waters/
            ripples growing dark
    covering the imprint
lying dormant,
            imagination failing
    this whole year.

                Year of miracles:
to have carried the mold all these months
                in the magnitude of space.
Now we had travelled to the edge

of the procession of peaks and valleys
would lead us to her flanks,
      trip to the rim of vision,
pointing always thru the overcast,
      remembrance of... a possibility
as a heliotrope fathoms the hidden sun.

Deep in waters, the mountain lay
wrapped in her veils and promises
ready to give herself from the feet up.

Foothills like an artist's workshop,
ochres, siennas, ambers,
draw the eye up to lose itself in blue heights,
dream of her radiance above our heads
weaving imperfect shades:
happy as children allowed to play
until light fades on hills around,
world of plants clinging to the tundra,
spreading outward like mats, sad as love-pangs,
wildflowers, short of summer warmth,
flickering energies on the bank,
      mosquito-murder in the greens
      "Lady, breathe your wind,
      move the dwarf-plants
      upon their fragile stems
      above our heads."

From the movement of
      a number of nearby stars
                we imagine that
a mountain becomes ours   from the depths
   conceived as bride
              from among the dead:
how stone mixes,
   slime firing in the kilns,
peaks claw skyward in some paroxysm,

folds settle in silence as for years
snow falls, cools into ice, flakes shrink,
lace tips melt
    and

eyes move
with a rush of birdwing
to see it: equanimity
       wings go, eyes stay
fuse with the contours of her limbs
      as the hills shake,
knees Ilex, elbows angle
    under a lapping tide and:
 suddenly
the great herds
emerge from the valley's end
hoofmarks on snow, churned up silks,
animals pouring like cataracts thru passes,
columns of swaying antlers
      cresting on skylines,
tatters of velvet like an army's banners
flying from pikes and lances,
the water mixed with snow and mud, waves
tan and grey as far as eye can see,
no start, no end: earth moves,
migrating North, driven by the shuffle of season,
nothing is steady underfoot, eyes quake
as the whole landscape floods.

  In the wind
     a fawn is dropped
   arrests the tide
  but momentarily,
      stopping the robe an instant
from sliding altogether
     to leave the mountain bare.

    Will the sun
thru interplay of cloud and weather
touch the mountain with a bridal flush
      or will she tonight
           recline in quiet greys,
                      a fading diva,
        whole camp as one
      facing in her direction
as she silently reads
      without stage effect
                  the poem of her life?

We   both here
in this process
        neither the outer
nor the inner suffer,
    the mountain
shaping our minds,
        and later, as the mind
gathers and shapes the mountain,
                 never loss.
In the dark,
      animal tides ripple still,
the night will not quench that flow but take it
              like a sea
from one end of the earth to the other.
                And not a moan,
not a wind whisper, but silence
              itself made motion
    on memory.
Gives the mountain back itself
      in marble tones
refraining from destruction
              of lesser things.

Until at last,
light on flank and crown,
            and death all lowered,
she stands revealed
wherever we would find ourselves within her country.
    Time speeds us to her encounter,
(human voices fading into the background)
        the whole range
                burns with white fire,
    Star among stars
whose radiance in the end
      comes to rest among men,
the taiga carpet receiving her,
      ponds and lakes catching her flare
            on this last day,
voices of birds and grasses
      crisscrossing in the night,
low hum of insects in the hells,
           memory stirring from its den,
    to try once more her storage.

III

God / Goddess

    Bride / Bridegroom

entailing,
    in each of our attitudes,
the best in me, which might be woman,
in you, which might be man.
    How will they tell,
who hear the poem of its life (the mountain's)
    which verse of it wrote which
and, following, who ended the stanza
            when eyes fell closed

in the dazzled tent
    whose blues and greens
                    we baptized at its knees?

As the light recedes
and takes from this frail universe
                        all terms of life,
    (leaves us in darkness
    most any planet could rush and occupy,
    ourselves, waking to morning in another world
        with no familiar maps)—
what a disconsolate place we inhabit
which could change out of recognition,
taking the seals of bride and bridegroom both
out of creation overnight, and leave us prey.

                    The stars
move like a tide over sleep,
    the cosmos,
            its peaks and seas
    in a procession:
                suddenly   (as one might put it):
                the great herds of stars
                    moving across the night   in silence
        without a moan, without apparent wind to move them,
            losing themselves completely
                                over the rim…

In the afterdark
    memory beginning to slip,
                        male thoughts,
        female thoughts,
            the small child thoughts,
                        like bannerets,
all going out at once, with starlight
            and the mountain also,
    reluctantly,

                        (its rock
                                    hardly awake to move, but
going over the edge also)
                                    and our storage
                                                without retrieval.

Knowing, or not, the plenitude: there is
                        no other question.
And, without forcing it:
                        the profundity.
            I collect stones, you
make your list of birds: we dredge
                                    the well of records.
When the page is full for the day,
            we can make love: this turn
will take me into manhood, you to womanhood,
                                                earth
shifting again underfoot
as if the hooves migrated thru our knees.
            This foursome
    of the implicit in each,
                bridal to the other,
and then the total other,
            strange at trail's end,
    of whatever sex,
            or of no sex whatever
(if the stars indeed have gone over and the world
            seethes with a new idea or two)
                    placing us both in question
                                and all identity.

This has to be a move,
retrieving the mountain,
in all its aspects,
translating it   /   an exhibition:
                the massive power now

  against
    the pity of it.
      The smallness, meanness,
  insignificance
      of all of it.
     Like destroying this land.
     This culture, however meagre.
     Making a laughing stock
 of this humanity.
     Ending Alashka
before it has begun.
      Deep in the well of darkness,
small flowers stir.
  They look at us, as a flower in Blake might do,
for a moment,
   the whole fate of our universe hangs on them:
      whether, tomorrow,
they are picked or not,
     trodden under foot or not,
        browsed or not,
by the tide of cattle.

     "How far we are from each other
     how close we are

     like a flower
     which cannot see itself
     and finds no mirror it can use
     in the clouded sky"

       IV

At the moment of strain,
     resolution
pushing up clouds off the valley floors
       makes

out of cloud a mountain:
>   (in our dreams
had we seen whale
>   above the waves
or waves themselves
>   (their blades of darkness?)

>   At the moment of strain,
   the killing time—
>   as if a sudden intruder,
in the middle of the poem
>   were to walk in, oblivious,
or if even you
>   were to touch me now
when the whole weight of it hangs in the balance,
or if this machine,
>   unable to bear the speed
of our attack on the mountain,
>   were to stumble, break down,
and lose the guiding thought—
>   so that the peak
could not loom above the cloud
>   as if it really were
in place, and not some play:
imagination under cloud   /
>   play   /   gamble

>   and one were sick
with a lurch of breath
>   into throat,
bile over tongue, nerves
>   shredded for the rest of the year:
   for memory
   would have blown connections
   and would not know
>   what lay behind the cloud.
   (Facing north,

or what we thought was north, waiting,
       for the mountain to come out
thinking there was something petty about the foothills,
but making nothing of it,
      (experts now),
        the mountain, hours later,
  like a trickster yet again,
    suddenly coming out to the northwest,
taking our breath away:
        immensity—
    but with a partial tallness,
    the summit in cloud now,
    the waistline open, but higher than
all height our memory had cradled.

IS IT THE MOUNTAIN LIES BEHIND THE CLOUDS, OR IS THE SUN…?

OR LOVE, THAT MOVES THE SUN AND OTHER STARS…?

         SOMETHING UNSAID AS YET…?

At the moment of strain,
      sleep meets waking
under the eyelids;
    the animals
flow in their tides over the hills,
their reins held firmly by the stars,
      washing themselves
on a dark tide
    over night-rocks:
      thought itself
a swell within the skull,
    linked to that movement
(backs of dolphin and whale)
    as if some stillness
      were the enemy.

  We have put up today
our defenses
    against oblivion.
       The mountain has put up
its longer argument.
  All definitions
hang in the balance.
      We are content
  to rest in every case.

Pendant to the Earth

I

We landed from the sky,
sea & earth
were sewn together,
a slant-eye
sealed shut
& behind its lid
we chuted down
in a dream
where fingers cracked
with sound of twigs,
our heads swivelling
on warm trunks,
scanning for sun.

Words protruded
from our mouths
like eggs
falling upon silence
& from these tiny spheres
small men stepped out
into prismatic air
carrying boats of eggshell white,
hand-sewn and silent boats
that make no rasp against the ice
& from the boats
a chain of animals paraded,
two by two,
just as we walked,
in two.

That was us,
in a photograph,

watching men leave town in boats
left behind with the women,
us in flight from tourists,
our shadow on the beach,
waiting for a chick
answering to the name of Beauty
as might be understood in these parts
if hailed by that name,
at best a luxury item
pushing her way
thru a swinging door,
braid at her back like a fin,
which of us would pay for her drink
and of us, what would she think,
and of our admiration?

II

That day,
almost everything was empty.
We stood at the edge
of human habitation
and ice regions
stretched beyond
the mind's boundaries,
stretched so far
they came round again.

That day,
we pressed our ears & lids to the earth
close as grass,
a life not quite
forgotten,
and grew as small as miniature plants,
tufts sprouting in our hair,
then shot up with long necks

to nuzzle the tops of mountains
and listen for the whisper of wolves
& news of passing herds,
we could have heard
a star drop
and mentioned it
with leaf-words, bone syllables,
rhythms that shook water
from wings, crests and bills.

III

Reading the snow after years
would tell
our direction, but nothing
makes for certain return
in a sudden whiteout
when shadows disappear,
contours flatten,
script erased by wind.
Snow would be
a warm bed
covering us with soft drifts
as even our hopes faded
like hills in fog,
cities of ice
we might reach,
skyscrapers of white on white
leaning away
at our approach.

There could be
no greater silence
than a crystal city
with no inhabitant
where even gulls are ivory.

To see a raven then,
his black our greatest gift,
to follow his track
until it made sense
or we made sense of it.

        IV

In memory,
"thought can embrace
any region whatsoever
    and in it
    and at will,
construct the setting
of some locus"
and while telling
about a place
we see two
written into a plain,
hands parting whaleribs
planted in a sacred oval,
range of greys
    clouds/ribs/mounds of snow,
there balanced on tussocks,
treading grass
turning nature's pages
with our feet
until we reach
that particular place
and not another,
that part of us
taking root at every moment
in where we are.

V

Imagine: our nation
its northern air
& words running east
towards the sun,
us waiting
in the shadow
of that door
to see them file by,
the hunters,
throbbing over ice,
the glare
as they close in
& the sun swings down
in a low arc
above the caps,
our bones inside flesh
rushing the mind's waters,
split off from land
two floes bobbing out to sea
lost in a memory
of white on grey.
Before the day
is snatched from our eyes
we wind towards the center
and disperse,
our bodies like tops
pause at the rim
then spin back to earth,
where we begin again
to know ourselves.

VI

Looking back
(walking softly over skulls
or shells
while the eider & puffin
speak to the sea
and the whales drive skyward
along the dog tongue beach
chewed at the edges
the sun
shoots thru a blue vein
to lagoons we cup in our palms,
a strange bird
black&white plumage mixed
swiftly passes
at dusk's grey moment.
Mirrors coated with tin
do not catch its passage
so swiftly it comes in
nor does anyone chance upon
its negative,
black where white was,
white where black,
nor the two birds
walking inside each other,
perpetually becoming one.

& between banks of ice
the water pulls at the boats,
that morning in summer when
calico women go out to the bluff
to sift thru layers of earth
for chips of bone & ivory
all from that same skeleton,
that earth-mound body,
and around the head,
hands swollen with cold

we also picked thru shards,
the skull bowl filling with light
while Beauty was
cool behind a pair of shades
& sneered over at us from the rim,
legs slightly apart
riding an invisible motorcycle,
hair streaming in the wind.

VII

When that landscape
    and we
have been split in two again
by the rays of the sun
& become
a pile of stones
made to look like men
& men hide behind us for the hunt,
& lichen grows on our lips
& we think
that all the creatures of the earth
are lying with their necks
across one another,
asleep like us,
& the snow begins to fall
in flakes,
white, light,
the fall of these flakes
forming layer on layer
the heart's power,
secretly like a mirror
separate from what it saw,
will have been
the eye behind a dream
suddenly flicked open,
that we may go and see our world!

Narrative of the Heartbeat

Lovely as birdflight
        above guns,
noise of hunt and war,
            boundaries,
over the sameness of mountains,
the abundance—
once you get into mountain country—
        the apparent
interminability of mountains, and their sameness,
           viewed from the car as we rush by,
              the colors
merging into one another,
blacks, furrow browns, greys, heathers:
        thigh-colors of goddess
where she parts to let sky in,
        where she parts to let rivers
    to allow to lakes
        their pleasures,

lovely as surmounting,
with the effortlessness,
        the distinguished ease
of the great flights of birds, launched
        at the wind like spears,
winged spears, with purposes they know alone
    but which to us
are purposeless and above criticism—
      no purer beauty than
          the contemplation
of the goddess moving,
          bird-skeins:
    her eyebrows as she comes towards us,
no purpose known to us
over the mountains

        the interminability
and apparent
      endlessness of the mountains,
yet I am on foot now,
     periploid,
feet bouncing in their boots
on the tussocks, your feet
       a few yards from mine
bouncing on the tussocks,
   we walk: alone / together
into the great wind of her breath,
as we move towards her or she
    towards us,
             no matter, as we move
   into each other
in the dazzle of this arctic morning
and I go
"Are those the so-and-so mountains over there,
is that the so-and-so range over there?"
    and we laugh after a while
because nothing ever moves in this country,

and your voice says,
laughing,
       "No, you don't have birdsight now,
   you are bewitched: look:
             that is not mountains you see there,
what you see is small pieces of ice
sticking out of the sea"
and I said "My God, I thought it was
at least the Brooks Range!"

and we continue
marching for insensate hours
into the channels of her throat,
into her nostrils,
down her ears,

into the caverns at the back of her glottis,
while, out there, in the world left behind,
her breasts are those hillocks,
her belly is this mountain over here,
that immense world-tree
(I know not its name here, but in Scandinavian
it is the central tree, the one we call Yggrasil—well,
      in any event)
that tree's umbrage is her pubis, and the branches
    her traps that she has between her lips
as we lick to her knees
    upturned, and thrash, and pant, to kiss
the long roots of her toes,

      messages, from outside:
mouse-peep, say, or chatter of ground squirrel,
    or, on parade, the wheatear,
come all the way from Scotland
        —(my own Norths, so far from home, so unforgotten)—
    and, sometimes, the traverse
of wolves scavenging the valleys
and, on high, the sheep picketing the snows,
and, in the middle, the caribou, choking in their thousands
        the immemorial passes...

but to look for the secret,
for the innermost wisdom,
for the velvet-pawed, soft-padding,
ghost who walks on molten sapphires among the tussocks,
you have to leave even your feet and set out into the dream
        of true, genuine, totally untouched
    wilderness,
and there you have to look into every bush,
    and detect
the direction of every drift in the sand along the riverbed,
the form of every stone in the bed
        and gauge its color and weight

and after you have been dreaming several hours,
    if fortune smiles,
and several days, if fortune smiles still,
        and a lifetime,
if fortune is still smiling and has not abandoned you,
    you may suddenly,
when no longer expecting it,
    when resigned,
when you have given up all but the last word
        it takes to remain alive, and when
you have perhaps given up hope for life and utter that last word
the one they call so mysterious, the name of the lady of these
        mountains,
then, on his velvet-pawed, soft-padding,
    mysterious way,
god-masked and tufted, come down at last to match
        that lady of the outermost mountains,
    with his fraternal eyes,
        so brotherly and blue, asking all his questions,
receiving all her answers, in her own communion,
        you may see at last

her heart's own master heartbeat, timid lynx.

So Long, the Kenai

    I

Nearing Kenai—
    city not peninsula—
difficult to find the city
    off the main road:
only two lines of churches

        to a dead god / the heart
we recognize at last:
        a shopping center about to be
in the mid-forest,
        side roads leading almost
nowhere, in the end:
        very last drop in the bucket,
old Russian chapel
        in a haze of golden grasses,
boarded up, (smelling of Novgorod),
        throttled
by squalid apartment blocks around it
they could have put anywhere else good grief
        in the green world.

        II

Nearing Homer,
        Ninilchik, native community,
"Help us protect our native way of life"
        (Orthodox church on the hill):
the fishermen stand at intervals
        as if voiding into the sea,
at the other end of town
        from the native-worked factory,
their campers in a neat line along the beach.
        They are trying to fish out
the heart of the great waters
        before it reaches the factory,
vein by bleeding vein:
        the salmon thrash like hearts
falling to pieces.

III

—Oil in Kachemak Bay?
—Oh I love the Bay but
—Do you love your Bay?
—Yes I love the Bay and
all the fish in it
        jumping
clear all the way from here
        into Cook Inlet,
but the big companies
are not men anymore,
        you know,
they are bigger than men and
you can't stop progress and
        the radical leader
in town has *too* many causes,
writes *too* many letters
about *too* many things and is
too radical about so much, add to
which he's not been here besides
what anyone would call around here
        very long.

IV

Freedom of the Spit
        living out three days
into the ocean
        bird-crossed, seal visited,
whale-visitationed.
        Ah the Bays, the Bays and Inlets
across the water!
        Boat bouncing out, the bosun's
bosom bouncing:
        local senator's kid, blonde, sassy.

Among the paradisal trees
        of the small haven,
State Senator, noblesse oblige,
            whistling in the warblers.
There is a wind, he says, I can't compete:
        there is no wind:
the birds surprisingly
        will not obey his laws
as well as men:
        Homer lost for oil, for pelf,
because the people fail to question
        the word *progress*.
Plato, at the end of his tether.
        A philosopher, white-bearded,
approaches the van,
        talks of selling out
his homestead
        or giving it away to someone
in the advancing hordes. Now the view has gone,
he smiles, what's the use of the money?

            V

The great scenic view
        is clouding over,
the rain drowns it out most days
        in any case:
soon the sludge will come down
        like the wrath of heaven
and drown it altogether.
        The killer whale
who has leaped his way
        up Cook Inlet
as far as Iliamna,
        leaps one last time
out of Eternity

        and stands sludge-bound
like a colossal
        semi-dipped cone
at a Dairy Queen's.
        Enchanted with free goodies,
the companies
        call for State Park
and Parking Lot, and Lottery:
        this / monument to vision.

VI

So long, the Kenai,
you will be sold for oil,
covered in hamburger joints
and denominational churches,
a spot of leprosy
from which no lupin spear,
no hemlock parachute,
and no black lily
        of Iliamna
can rise or fall—
sold to men, mud, mosquitos,
to buy a little respite
for all the rest
until the rest also
dies of the plague.
Alashka, U.S.A.
"North to the Future!"
The Future of What?

Letter from Homer

Down by Homer
        with the wind at too many knots
blowing away the tent,
        the thought seizes me again
            why do I not go out
in the dark blue ship
    whose horn is blowing in the harbor
                straining to sea,
  and loose myself
from this Ithaca with whom I am
    so uneasily re-united,
the traveller's blood
             leaping like salmon
       in every vein?

            Yesterday
there were no black lilies opposite Iliamna
              tho, after rain,
    just as I got to Homer,
all the mountains rose at once out of the mist
            to bow to me
     with a white dazzle.
           Travel within
  travel: I move without moving,
   having seen these lands before,
with the needling of discovery
            in every pore,
so that, now, Ithaca has become familiar
straining forward like a ship on the waters
             and I am contracted
for years to come,
       a wanderer.

          This was to be
a staying time for us, where you and I

would sit at home for once
(provisionally, a forward base of home)
                        and work these poems
to viability.
            Instead, we are at letters again.
            Everything moves.
            I move from Anchorage,
            you move to Hope,
            I should go next, in this chessgame,
            to somewhere like Ultima Thule
            under the setting sun.
            When you go, I arrive,
            when you arrive, I move
            even tho the mind stumbles
            and comes to a halt.

Which is what it might have meant after all,
that story of the man supposedly satisfied
by his return to the home he had left for so long,
his winning the contest of the great bow,
decimating the stars of Greece, his rivals,
his toes licked by dogs and nurses,
his bed graced by the flower of wives,
                        when he heard
the loud song of the ship in the harbor
    calling to sea,   THALASSA!   THALASSA!
                  knowing he went,
already as the ship strained for the sea,
                into a calm
    more terrible than the calm of sirens
                  and that the rock
he felt anchored to, unable to really move,
    as the ship plunged down to doom,
                  —they would call it
Purgatorio, or America, no matter:
                  it was that stone
the mind became which had begun to slow.

Three Death Poems

I

Death comes
to the iceman
(with knowledge of ice,
slowly)
bristles on the surf,
the waves of his thoughts
turning white
& the sun dips north,
sparks of water
salt his tongue,
his eye skates inward
to a zone of sharpness
& there he watches
the broad flukes
of leviathan sounding,
& overhead
shadows sweep,
& points of light,
as he moves thru the dusk
following the eider and whale.

II

I remember
you ask:
what is this?
what is this?
what sort of place
have I been living in
all these years,
I who was born
to live in Paradise
and not this place?
Not Paradise,
not these children
whining for food,
thin rations
you eat with guilt,
old man
since the last born
your place inside
the house has shrunk,
you swallowed it one day
with the air
in your food.

So that night
you leave
your hunting skins
by your grandson's head.

They hear you go out,
door slams behind
wind holds it shut,
& you are blown
praying to lose

your eyesight,
your face warmed
by a fall of feathers,
the snow's burn
against your cheeks:
light of the place
you feel you should have lived in
all your long life.

They'll find you
in the spring,
your body white
as Paradise.

III

The vow
of the sealskin rope,
would you take it,
if I asked you
some afternoon in spring
when wildflowers huddle
close to the ground
would you come
to my tent if I asked you
& help me tie
the ends of a rope
up on the ridgepole,
loop hanging down
two feet from the floor,
would you help me
put on my clothes,
without reproaches
would you help me
sit my ageing frame
down beside the rope,
my head
through the loop
like I asked
would you hurry
to press down
the back of my head,
would you
on a sunlit afternoon
while the whales
spout offshore
help an old friend
and mate these past years
until she was dead?

A great deal of talk on the "mystery" of being
Native. In the end, we ask X how she can keep together
in her head i) the "mystification" of her culture as a
Native, and ii) the axiom that nothing need remain un-
elucidated by the science she practices. There is no
answer.

They worry about the non-Native ripping off the
Native and the Native himself ripping off his own people.
Some of these Natives are poets: we try to discuss the
poet, a Prometheus, the great thief of fire who has
never been held responsible for the provenience of his
sources. How can you copyright anything in the ideological
realm? How can the balance be found, in *any* culture,
between possession and non-possession, between Marx and
the Buddha?

The Natives have a unique land settlement deal
with the Feds but it leaves them wide open to the sell-
and-be-sold ethic of the nation. Indeed, as patriotic
nationals, this is what they claim themselves to have
desired. But they are being pushed into "Progress,"
"Originality" and "Evolution" when the issue of these
is in all likelihood already decided by the system.
What the Natives seem to fear is whether or not they
have the energy, and the genius, to save themselves
and us also. Sublime irony of the Union: to have pushed
the original Americans into being the Saviors. Would
anyone in this position not die laughing?

V

THE FOREST 2

You set out over that glacier
with nothing to eat,
it's a long way to walk
with no food.

You think you see
a wolverine,
use it as a compass
you walk towards it
& as you get closer
the wolverine
becomes a little hill,
the closer you get
the more it becomes
a little island
coated with trees.

Come night you build a fire,
prepare for sleep hungry
but a wolverine
is drawn to the flames
& you kill—
its flesh you cut up
& pass around
like Jesus the loaves
so none will go hungry.

Next day you walk on
& see a little rabbit,
use it as a compass
you are walking towards it
& as you get closer
the rabbit
becomes a mountaintop.

You come like Moses out of Egypt,
out of a fight/starvation/war
bringing your people with you,
taking a name from the land,
wherever you settle.

You come across a bird
the bird
doesn't want
to be killed
so in place of its life
it gives you its song
& you listen
until you have it
by heart.

You come across a beaver
the beaver
doesn't want
to be killed
so in place or its life
it gives you its song
& you listen
until you have it
by heart,
and so on
with all the animals
until you have them
all by heart.

Return of the Raven:
You think the ship
is a great bird
& take to the woods,
you spy on it
thru tubes
of rolled skunk cabbage leaf.
When the sails
are made fast
it is as if
the bird
has folded its wings.
You imagine a flock of crow
flies out from the rigging.

It keeps happening
just like that
you are so alone
but keep walking
on that glacier
& always see
a man coming
& get there
every time
he disappears.
You even dress up to meet him,
but every time
he's never there.

A bird
all the time
flies around you
pecks your face
wakes you up
& in yr. anger
you club the bird
knock it down
you are so restless
& cannot sleep & the bird
you knock down
is your sleep.

You walk along the beach
gazing at little rocks,
looking for something,
each time
all you see
is little rocks,
you give up hope
of ever seeing it

& look at the rocks,
waiting for sleep.

In your songs
lots of men
are coming towards you
& yr. sleep
flies down,
encasing you
with its wings.

Time of sickness,
the deaths
are coming fast
you don't look
& when one dies,
just sits there,
mothers with babies
in their arms, so many,
when you burn them
the air is thick as smoke.

Charcoal along the ground
you poke
with spearhead of driftiron
burn them
& put the ashes
in a little house
on posts.

You go for light
& all you see
is eyes of dead bodies
shining like sparks
you kindle them on the beach
so they'll never
turn to ground.

All your family dies
only your uncle is left
& he nurses you
from his own breast,
he doesn't know
what on earth to do
so he gives you his breast,
and you are raised
on your uncle's breast.

You hear your father
singing in the waves
& one night
he marches in,
you're going to be lucky,
you're not going
to be broke, your father
is going to take
care of you. Tosses
a fish you can catch
& money flows toward you
like silver scales.

Your father sleeps
inside your dream,
the bad dreams
you kill
by talking them into
a jar in the morning.

When they bring your father in
lifeless from the sea
she takes his hand
lays it on her breast,
a silent wish.
Eight times
around the pyre
then digs a path
& squats
for his spirit
to come in.

She was afraid
she'd lose you as a boy
that just at birth
you'd be a girl,
private parts
breaking open & stuff
running out
& people saying
"his place below
became female."
So she called upon his spirit
to enter her.

& yr. mother
called you her
little husband.

Your wife says to you:
the world was turning with our breath
& now the feather is still
that once moved
with that world.
You always get sorry about things
so I don't tell you
some pieces are rotting
from our house.

Already they have opened the door
& we stand outside
at the corner,
our blankets thrown down,
waiting for them
to toss food to us
in the fire,
inside,
where the fire sparks
each time
we speak,
since they no longer
can hear us.

You hunt together,
you are great hunters,
your dog leads you
you follow
to see why
he's barking.
You see him
running on the snow,
keeps on barking,
you never catch up,
keep on going,
he keeps on
running and barking,
to that place
the other side of the sky,
where you come to the lightning,
when the tide is out
a body's length.

You've got
a big story
on that crow:
he's like Superman
or the Christchild,
born in moss,
    lowly
not in furs.

The little lakes are
water dripping
from his mouth
the little drops
run out the sides
of his beak
he is the rock
his mother swallowed,
down there the sea
grinds its teeth in sorrow,
the surf dashing in
among the boulders,
a clam-spitting place
at low tide.

His stories
are like the Bible only
he's a bird
who made lakes
and people and told
the animals
where to go.
He thought of poor people
who can't afford furs
& wouldn't get born
until they brought him

some moss.
This is the way
it always starts:
it bothers you,
hiding inside
your body,
gives you
mostly troubles.
You get sick,
& get strong.
You are infected
with his spirit,
hiding inside.

It's the special time
of care, for days
you don't take food
or drink.
It's early morning,
wintertime.
Back home your wife,
stealing water
makes a big river
in the woods
across your path.
She's so thirsty
she can't help it
she spills some,
makes a big river.
But you don't
lose your power,
you get across,
you and your dog,
leaving tracks
in the snow.
It's wintertime,
river's frozen.

People rowing around
in space
in the air
over there
you see these boats
rowing towards you
thru the air.
You sit down
upon a log, don't know
what to do,
jump up,
start running
pretty soon
they're all around,
they put their paddles
back and forth
then pretty soon
the sun comes round
to that position
where the canoes
are coming in,
driving at your heart.

You die for four days,
your crying wife & kids
watch the body.
First day,
you make a noise
second day,
you make a noise
& in four days
you're back
from that place
on the shore
where you saw—
a big black boat
with sails and—
lots of people on it.

Museums can be a source of great joy. They preserve and enhance objects as carriers of knowledge. They bring and keep together the great apparatus of scholarship. They favor the compilation of history.

Museums are also prisons for objects. They legitimize robbery on an almost unimaginable scale.

Let us work towards the end of this vast exile of matter. Bring back the heads, the hands, the torsos, the pictures, the manuscripts, the furnishings, the weapons, the pots and containers, the gifts and the tools to their original places of emergence. Then travel would once again be meaningful. One could go to a whole Egypt, a complete Italy, an entire Northwest Coast.

There might be an Alashka.

Archeologists could begin by explaining to the people among whom they dig what it is they are doing and why. We could build homes for the fruits of the ground on that selfsame ground, instead of hauling them away to foreign stores. Then, perhaps, the people would live alongside their own past and honor it instead of imitating us by selling it.

Narrative/Invocation of, and to, the Place Klukwan

After months of stubble:
    green trees,
sky-spears,
    everything vertical,
jagged now,
        the raven over all.

    I am a child
eighteen or so—
    no one has paid enough
attention to me as a child,
        least of all myself.
Trying to reach
    outside my frame,
some otherness:
well, my old teacher, the Great Jew,
raven of France,
    in love with such as these,
reading his Asdiwal:
        found rock at sea,
    hero in middle,
caught between earth and sky:
           and / well:
what *should* poor fellows as I do,
        nicht wahr,
    but follow?

    Now I am here.
Alaskan Airlines pamphlet:
"How to look at Totems."
    "Village of Klukwan
        northernmost
    outpost of Thlingeet

    Chilkat River
  some of the finest
    houseposts & housescreens
 in all Alaska."

Village about as silent as most.
Streets virtually deserted.
Middle of main street,
old lady being helped into a car
just as we get there.
We had an introduction from a friend
(most beautiful American woman)
to her grandmother
(oldest American woman)
who makes the last Chilkat blankets
(American)
at the village of Klukwan.
Our stars are dead.

Just before Haines,
 roadside cemetery:
one tomb with a Thlingeet bear,
 one with the Star of David.
You could, Klukwan,
 with your Jewish names
in this Protestant idyll,
 convert to Judaism wholesale
and confound the neighbors!
 Do it for good, nicht wahr?
(I should write to the Chief:)

   "Klukwan,
   you could accommodate
   those famous housescreens
   and charge the Wasp a mint
   when he came by to see them!
   Klukwan,

stone faces Klukwan,
dog in the manger Klukwan
with the big bone
you cannot use,
the big bone rotting
in its trough unseen
either by you
or other men,
because the museums
all over the world
are full of Klukwan
(and the chief
who took the Klukwan things
died mysteriously).

Dead new houses
without eyes,
fluorescent lighting
never turned on,
and the streets,
the paralysis!
The synagogues of Poland,
also of wood,
exist only
in photographs now,
and you, Klukwan,
sitting on
the useless bone,
the wood rotting,
the masks leaking
out of their eyes,
drowning out
the legends…

You people
with the names of Jews
and the last secrets

of goat-hair property,
how just it is
that I should pay
for my fathers' sins
who paid for
the sins of theirs!
Right, Klukwan?
Do not the Jews refuse
to speak to the Germans
and do you not refuse,
with your German Jewish fathers,
to speak with us?

   —all white men of one face,
     with stone eyes,
     of whom no questions are asked,
     to find out their kind,
     with never the right shade of eyes,
     whose eyes, if blue, shld. be brown,
     whose eyes, if brown, shld. be blue,
     ghosts,   all ghosts
            after the great destruction?"

I have dreamed of this place twenty-five years,
            so long
even my dreams are historical.
           The omens
have not been good: this block at Klukwan.
             We shall discuss it
all down the coast, get explanations,
how many whites came by to take out Klukwan,
how every day offers are made for Klukwan.
Down the coast they are making plans,
building museums for Klukwan and suchlike places
but Klukwan doesn't send its things to museums,
nor make a museum for itself.
              Down the coast, the poles die also,

the great poles lie rotting in the forests
unvisited by anyone, except rats and beavers,
shown no kindness by anyone, no remembrance.

  When it could have been so beautiful, after all,
     the mumbling over,
  the invitation out that everyone should join the clan!
     But the suffering:
          too long.
     And that *pride*

          The matter of Klukwan
sticks like a fishbone in my throat.
     the anxiety…
       is terrible.

In plain language.

On Emerging from a Writers' Conference in Alashka:

What, if anything, have the Native artist and the non-Native artist to say to each other?

First: there is a group of Native artists, now, in Alashka, who are artists first and foremost, and secondarily "Native artists." They are asking many questions. They ask what is their relation to the Native traditions from which they arise and their tradition-bearers. They ask—being, often, city folk now—what is their relation to the villagers in their home areas, many of whom are working in "folk" or "pop" traditions, frequently degenerating into "airport" art. Do they still have anything to do with the little ivory bears or the little wooden totem poles found in every gift-shop in the State? In another direction, they ask what is their relation to other artists: Native artists outside Alashka, in the rest of America, in the rest of the Third World—eventually the body of universal art itself.

But it may be too easy for a non-Native artist to describe things this way. He says: "Art is universal, give us yours, give yours to the world." The Native may feel he has given too much already. The museums of the world are full of Native art, much of which was stolen, not given. Are there Native museums full of Native art? Are there Native museums full of world art? Are there *any* museums of world art in Alashka? How many world artists are coming to Alashka to give and exchange? Few or none. Has Native ownership of Native art—most Alashkan peoples have had, and still have, strong senses of copyright—been respected? No. Not even by anthropologists, artists, writers. They take these things, put them in their museums, their houses, their books; they teach them, make careers out of them. Ourselves included. It is enough to induce despair in Native and non-Native artists alike. Or anger, and the determination to take back into Native hands the ownership and leadership of ALL Native art wherever it may be. In such senses, the non-Native, including the non-Native artist, can only do one thing. Get out of the way. Self-destruct.

It is also true that most artists, everywhere, have always been ripped off. What the Native and the non-Native artists may have to say to each other is this. In many senses, we believe in the same things. We are one race and this race is the oldest race of all, beyond "race," beyond "color," beyond "sex," beyond all such divisions. It has always been exploited everywhere, at all times. If we can look to that, remember that, there is still time, on this one mother earth, to forget the crimes we have committed against each other as humans and hold to the love we might have for each other as artists, poets, singers.

To give, to accept, to exchange, to share, to celebrate, to praise.

VI

THE ROAD OUT

Perimeter

His great flipper pierces the water
and lands with a slap.
For miles the message travels:
Slap, the flags, slap, the cannon,
Slap, the blue suits standing in line
small as dolls, eyes & buttons
shining in the wind,
as, slap, for no reason,
from a distance a people
watching flags on a pole,
listens to the squeak of brass music,
guns over ancestral waters,
glides away silent, slap,
with no say in the matter.

Marching Orders

We are at the entrance of the great
        Pacific Northwest Coast.
Far up a street in Skagway,
        a street nobody travels,
a very ordinary house,
        a very ordinary window,
a sign in very small letters:
        "Go back to Boston."

What We Have Known As the Northwest Is the Southeast

From the top of the tree
where we had climbed in hope of,
in hope of what, we ask,
the skull at the top of the spine,
ravens at both windows,
pecking us out,

we fell out of Alashka
in a rush of rain,
flushed out by cataracts,
unending rushes of water
greening the pines and ferns,
into the sun-drenched fruit bowls,

after three weeks of rain,
no longer sure of the outlines
of leaping fish, or mountain
smoking at dawn as mist burns off,
common or garden sunlight
is like a god-gift.   Raven?

On the last day up there,
at the top of the tree,
drank wine on a big Englishman,
bought the flag of Alashka,
found antique ivory to cherish
and, after beer and love,

for the first time in our joint life,
we danced,
we danced in Ketchikan…

Oregon Coast

Disposition of the rocks at sea,
immense meditation gardens:
        lines of the waves
hesitating at rocks,
        providing *paseos* for whales
moving thru patient courtship—
        their meditation as they select
mates on the long voyage
        at leisure till Baja
(down from Alashka)
        to flirt & browse—

the immense rock gardens,
the promenades,
the mammals breathing,
a patience we no longer know,
depths they are still in touch with
        thru the veins of water

Redwoods

If there be tree-spirits
these are the homes of archangels,
thrones, dominations.

        Will America last,
once tall as these?
        After Alashka,
we neglect the sights,
        except for giants.

It happens: redwoods (California),
        dinosaurs (Utah-Colorado).

These trees should have been in Southeast.
Can you imagine what the Thlingeet
would have made of them?
They would have gone bananas
over totem poles
skyscraper-high!

      We shrink by the minute
among these trees
      but are not in any way
diminished by them.

Tactic

The question
of remembering it
will always be:
(& how is it
that we can walk
upon this earth
for so long
& not know
how long
or when
or how many times
we will come back
or what form
we will take,
if,
in the high peaks

of the Alashka Range,
we will fall like snow
before the ice
begins to move,
or if a glacier
flowing downhill
into warmer climes
will evaporate us,
not knowing,
or having forgotten
that we were
just you and me
that summer,
driving along the vastness
of the American continent.
BELIEVING
WHAT WE SAW
TO BE REAL?

Home from the Nightless Summer

The world has fallen down:
we are the only ones
        who remember how it was
made,   put together.
        Entering night again,
we must hold onto each other,
no other memory is left.
        We are the plan,
time's grid,
        & no one else survives.
Like: the sea's whisper
is the great land's name in our ears,

                Alashka
      like: the shape of waves is
its mountain shoulders
                    Alashka—
      distantly, haunted,
we remember its beauty,
the noise of those glaciers
                folding their arms…

Loving the sharp green of dwarf plant colonies on dark sand, in a dark light.

Another very beautiful thing: the wind rotates the tip of a grass blade around its own base so that it draws a perfect circle in the sand.

In that wind we hear the name.

Note from the Authors

In 1974, Janet Rodney and Nathaniel Tarn, who had met at Rutgers University, had begun to live together on the Delaware River separating Pennsylvania from New Jersey, began a three year series of long summer sojourns in Alaska, a state they soon found to be the most beautiful of all North American lands.

A wooden bed opening up into a storage box was made and mounted into Rodney's Dodge 200 van. Tarn went first up though the northern territories into Canada. Rodney flew and met him at St. George in the Yukon after which they drove the Alcan Highway to the Alaskan border and on to Anchorage. In this season and subsequent ones, they traveled the whole state in the van, camping in places like the S.E. forests, the Homer spit; several glaciers and the mighty Mount Denali park. They took ship on every single ferry in the Alaskan fleet. They flew up to the Arctic shore and out to the islands in the Bering Sea. They lived in university dorms, in Inuit village schools, in private houses lent to them short-term by Indigenous men and women. During one summer, they took part in a Literary Conference with the likes of Edward Dorn. The last voyage consisted of Tarn teaching Arctic anthropology to tourists on the *Lindblad Explorer* all the way thru the Aleutians as far as Hokkaido. The coming and going involved many kinds of travel: one, for example, sent the pair all the way thru Indigenous villages (studying totem poles) to the Eastern Canadian cities.

Given that both were poets and would probably write on the road; given also the problematic attitudes of the establishment as late as the mid-seventies toward joint writing of an experimental nature by two people, especially a man and woman together, Tarn and Rodney opted to create a book making use of their individual words joined together as one experimentally different voice. The result of "one voice, two authors" was summed up in the Acknowledgements to the first edition as follows:

> "Despite any kind of appearances, every single poem in this geography is a jointly created fiction and any resemblance between the voices you hear and real, flesh and blood authors is purely coincidental."

This is followed by an offering of the work to "the real voices of several people," naming some twenty Indigenous friends as well as "earlier geographers" like Boas, Carpenter, Lévi-Strauss *inter alia*. Quite deliberately the two authors have never discussed in any way or form the procedures followed in getting this creation together and do not intend to. Of course, there are many letters, diaries, journals and general references to the trips in the writers' archives.

The work has had a difficult history. It eventually landed in the hands of a person who owned a bookstore in Boulder, Colorado and who was interested in trying his hand at publishing. A major problem: this was 1979 and Tarn and Rodney were leaving for a year's anthropological fieldwork in Santiago Atitlán, the Guatemalan village in which Tarn had done his doctoral work in 1952-3 and to which he had returned in 1969. As a result the book was taken out of the authors' hands. Friend and filmmaker David Lenfest, they seem to recall, suggested to the publisher that the *Alashka* be joined to a selected poems of Tarn's and this made the book into *Atitlán/Alashka* sent into the world by Brillig Works, Boulder, during their absence. It met with no especial reception and disappeared from view. As is well known, attitudes shifted dramatically shortly after *Alashka* was written. Many years later, Tarn discovered that a few copies had been living under the publisher's bed and the Boulder gentleman very kindly sent those on. They are stored in New Mexico with the two authors.

Only two comments on the book are recorded. A young, aspiring Tlingit poet friend in Alaska took great exception, for reasons incomprehensible, to the presence of "a woman" in the joint work. A shocking statement when you consider that the kinship system of the Tlingit is matrilineal. Note too it wasn't until 1975 that Frederica de Laguna and Margaret Mead were elected into the National Academy of Sciences, the first women in the field of anthropology to receive that honor.

At some point, well after their travels, Tarn—in an unusual and exceptional way—wrote to a rather conventional, old-school American poet living in Alaska asking him whether he could not give some help in making the book known in his state. In a microscopic reply, this poet replied that he found the language unacceptably "garrulous" (we believe this was the word used); the intended significance is not in doubt.

Tarn and Rodney both continue to feel that since there are no uncountable masses of worthwhile literary writing on Alaska that they know of, their book, on its own for the first time, might now conceivably gain an audience in the place which gave it birth as well as in other places on this globe.

www.ingramcontent.com/pod-product-compliance
Lightning Source LLC
Chambersburg PA
CBHW022114160426
43197CB00009B/1025